I would like to dedicate this book to everyone in the UK who has extended the hand of friendship, made me feel welcome, and helped me to integrate my cultural identity. My heart is now here with the British people and, without a doubt, London is my home. This has been my home now for twenty years, and it has been the most incredible time, so thank you all.

Thank you also to everyone I have met in my twenty-five years as a chef, and to my mum, Isabel, my soulmate, Peter, and all of my family and friends.

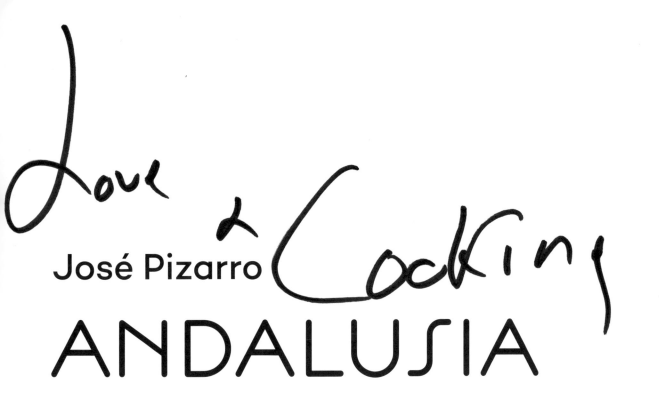

Love & Cooking

José Pizarro

ANDALUSIA

Recipes from
Seville and beyond

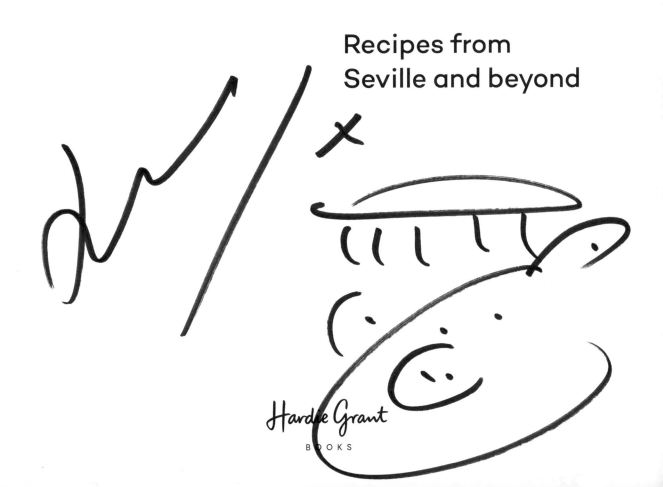

Hardie Grant
BOOKS

Contents

Introduction

As the southernmost region of Spain, Andalusia, with its wealth of fertile farmland, vertiginous mountain ranges and rugged yet abundant coastline, is one of the most gastronomically unique, and rich, areas of the country. I have travelled here more times than I can remember; from my very first childhood holidays at the beach, to explorations of the restaurants of Seville and beyond. During the research of this book, I learnt so much about the culture and its strong Moorish and Roman heritage, which you see reflected in everything from architecture to everyday food. But I learned a lot about the people, too – it seems to me that everyone is always happy, and most have an incredible sense of humour! The wonderful light and good weather have an effect on the mood, of course, but I tend to think it has something to do with the unquestionably good food, too.

Andalusian cuisine is dictated by the fish in the sea, the animals in the fields and the wilds of the mountains, and the fruit and vegetables grown in orchards and gardens. Divided into eight provinces, each has its own traditional dishes and desserts, and in many cases, their own claim to the recipes that have made the region famous. My aim is to take you on an amazing journey, from the beaches of the south west to the desert in Almería, and across the historical cities, beautiful mountain ranges and hidden towns – cooking incredible food along the way.

MEAT

Eating happy, healthy, free-range animals is of paramount importance in Andalusia; in this region, you can find *dehesas* – woodlands – where Ibérico pigs eat acorns that have fallen from the trees and roam freely for many kilometres every day. The charcuterie and meat, jamón Ibérico, is renowned for its high-quality fat. Walking around the *dehesas* in Córdoba and Huelva, observing how these animals live, is one of the things that relaxes me the most.

Due to the varied climate, a result of the mountain ranges, the area also has great game, and I really enjoy cooking with it.

Slow-cooked oxtail

Serves 4 with leftovers for
Oxtail croquetas (page 20)

This is one of the most traditional dishes in Seville, and you'll be able to find it in restaurants all over the city, but particularly in places near the bullfighting ring. I use Palo Cortado sherry in a lot of recipes instead of red wine, as I find its flavour richer and deeper. I love this type of sherry so much, I have produced my own, and I even recently visited my good friends at Moser Glassworks in the Czech Republic to design my own sherry glass. When I was there, I was blown away by their passion and dedication to their craft. Every single piece is made by hand using traditional methods that are hundreds of years old, much like the art of producing sherry – making them perfect partners.

2 tablespoons lard or Ibérico
   pork fat
2 kg (4 lb 6½ oz) oxtail, cut into
   large chunks
sea salt and freshly ground
   black pepper
1 onion, chopped
1 carrot, chopped
1 celery stalk, chopped
2 tablespoons tomato purée
1 teaspoon sweet smoked
   pimentón de la Vera
1 teaspoon hot smoked
   pimentón de la Vera
200 ml (7 fl oz/¾ cup)
   Palo Cortado sherry
400 g (14 oz) tin chopped
   tomatoes
1 litre (34 fl oz/4 cups) chicken
   stock

To serve
bread, chips and a nice bottle
   of red or Palo Cortado sherry

In a heavy-based, lidded saucepan or casserole dish, warm 1 tablespoon of the lard over a medium-high heat, until melted. Meanwhile, season the oxtail with salt and pepper. When the lard is hot, add the meat to the saucepan, brown on all sides, then remove and set aside.

Reduce the heat to medium and melt the rest of the lard in the saucepan. Fry the onion, carrot and celery, until softened but not browned, around 5–8 minutes. Stir in the tomato purée and both types of pimentón and cook for 1 minute, until fragrant. Add the sherry with the browned oxtail and simmer to reduce it by half, about 5–10 minutes.

Pour in the chopped tomatoes and stock, bring to a boil, then turn down to a gentle simmer. Cook, covered, for 2½ hours, then remove the lid and cook for a further 30–40 minutes to reduce the braising liquid.

The leftovers are best used for croquetas, for which you'll need about 250 g (9 oz) meat.

Oxtail croquetas

Makes 24

At the restaurants, we are always experimenting with croquetas, trying to come up with different flavours and textures. By far the best results seem to come from using leftovers – and this is a perfect example.

250 g (9 oz) Slow-cooked oxtail (page 18)
½ teaspoon hot smoked pimentón de la Vera
½ teaspoon tomato purée
sea salt and freshly ground black pepper
400 ml (13 fl oz/1¾ cups) whole (full-fat) milk
100 ml (3½ fl oz/½ cup) strong beef stock
80 g (2¾ oz) butter
75 g (2½ oz/generous ½ cup) plain (all-purpose) flour
50 g (1¾ oz/½ cup) hazelnuts or walnuts, finely ground
2 large free-range eggs, beaten
125 g (4½ oz/1⅓ cups) dry breadcrumbs
olive oil or sunflower oil, for deep-frying

Shred the cooked oxtail in a bowl and mix with the hot smoked pimentón and tomato purée. Check the seasoning, adjusting if necessary and set aside.

To make the béchamel, warm the milk and stock together in a saucepan over a medium heat. In a separate saucepan, melt the butter over a medium heat, stir in the flour and cook for 2–3 minutes, until the mixture starts to brown. Stir in the ground nuts, turn the heat down slightly and add the milk and stock little by little, stirring continuously and pouring in more as it thickens, until you have a smooth and silky béchamel sauce.

Add the shredded oxtail mixture and stir well to combine. Season generously with salt and pepper.

Spread the mixture onto a shallow tray and press a sheet of cling film (plastic wrap) over the top to stop a skin from forming. Chill in the fridge for at least 2 hours, until firm.

Lightly grease your hands with olive oil or water and roll the mixture into 30 g (1 oz) balls. If they are a little soft, put them on a tray in the freezer for 30 minutes to firm up.

Place the beaten egg and the breadcrumbs into two separate bowls. Using one hand, dip a croqueta into the egg, then use the other hand to roll it in the breadcrumbs until evenly coated. Place on a tray, and repeat until you have breaded all the croquetas.

Heat 2 cm (1 in) oil in a deep saucepan to 180°C (350°F) – or until a cube of bread browns in about 20 seconds – and fry the croquetas in batches for around 2 minutes, or until golden. Drain on paper towels, then eat immediately.

Pollo empanao & tomato salad

Serves 4

Whether served hot or cold, this is one of my favourite things to eat. I have fond memories of travelling from my hometown in Extremadura to Cádiz for my summer holidays with my uncles, taking this for a picnic along the way. You can also use this marinade for salmon, lamb or vegetables on the barbecue; the lemon in it caramelises beautifully.

4 free-range boneless skinless chicken breasts
2 garlic cloves, bashed
50 ml (2 fl oz/¼ cup) extra-virgin olive oil
100 ml (3½ fl oz/scant ½ cup) white wine
zest and juice of 1 lemon
sea salt and freshly ground black pepper
3 tablespoons plain (all-purpose) flour
2 large free-range eggs, beaten
75 g (2½ oz/¾ cup) fine dry breadcrumbs
sunflower or olive oil, for shallow frying

For the lemon mayonnaise
2 free-range egg yolks
sea salt and freshly ground black pepper
finely grated zest of 1 lemon and a squeeze of juice
250 ml (8½ fl oz/1 cup) light olive oil
2–3 tablespoons extra-virgin olive oil

Sandwich each chicken breast between two sheets of cling film (plastic wrap). Using a rolling pin, gently bash the chicken breasts so each flattens to 1 cm (½ in) thick, trying not to break the flesh. Remove the cling film and place into a large ceramic or glass dish.

Whisk the garlic, olive oil, wine and lemon zest and juice together in a small jug or bowl, then season well. Pour over the chicken, making sure it is evenly coated. Cover and marinate in the fridge for at least 1 hour, but preferably overnight.

To make the mayonnaise, whisk the egg yolks with some salt and pepper and the lemon zest. Gradually add the light olive oil in a steady stream, whisking constantly, until you have a thick mayonnaise. Whisk in the extra-virgin olive oil and add lemon juice to taste.

When you are ready to cook the chicken, put the flour, egg and breadcrumbs into three separate shallow bowls. Shake off any excess marinade, then dip each breast into the flour, followed by the egg, then finally the breadcrumbs, until evenly coated. Set aside.

To make the salad, arrange the tomato slices on a serving platter. Scatter with the garlic and plenty of salt and black pepper. Whisk the white wine and vinegar with a little seasoning in a small jug or bowl, then whisk in the olive oil. Pour over the tomatoes and set aside.

For the tomato salad

1 kg (2 lb 3 oz) very ripe vine
    tomatoes, sliced
3 garlic cloves, minced
sea salt and freshly ground
    black pepper
50 ml (2 fl oz/¼ cup) white wine
2 teaspoons sherry vinegar
5 tablespoons extra-virgin olive
    oil, for drizzling

Pour 2 cm (1 in) oil into a wide, deep frying pan over a
medium-high heat. Once the oil is shimmering, fry the
breaded chicken for 5–7 minutes on each side until golden
and cooked through – this will depend a little on how thick
the chicken breasts are. You may need to fry in batches,
depending on the size of the pan. Place on kitchen paper
to absorb any excess oil, then serve warm with the lemon
mayonnaise and tomato salad. Alternatively, allow to cool
then wrap in baking paper to eat later with the lemon
mayonnaise and tomato salad.

Slow-cooked pork cheeks with Oloroso sherry

Serves 6–8

Pork cheeks generally are a flavourful cut, but when you try cheeks from Ibérico pigs, you will really notice the difference. Being acorn fed, the animals have very strong jaw muscles in order to break down the hard shells with their teeth.
In addition, the oil from the acorns gives the meat a much richer, nuttier taste.

1.5 kg (3 lb 5 oz) pork cheeks, preferably Ibérico, cleaned and trimmed
150 g (5 oz) jamón Ibérico, cubed
750 ml (25 fl oz/3 cups) Oloroso sherry
1 carrot, chopped
1 onion, finely sliced
2 garlic cloves, unpeeled, bashed
1 bay leaf
2 sprigs of rosemary, finely chopped
3 black peppercorns
sea salt and freshly ground black pepper
2–3 tablespoons olive oil, for frying
300 ml (10 fl oz/1¼ cups) chicken stock

To serve
crusty bread

Place the pork cheeks and jamón Ibérico in a glass or ceramic dish. Pour over the sherry, add the carrot, onion, garlic, bay leaf and peppercorns. Cover and leave to marinate in the fridge for at least 8 hours, preferably overnight.

Drain and reserve the marinade liquid and aromatics from the vegetables, jamón and pork cheeks. Pat the meat dry with kitchen paper and season well.

Pour the oil into a heavy-based, lidded saucepan or casserole dish. Fry the pork cheeks on all sides over a medium-high heat until well browned and caramelised, about 1-2 minutes on each side. Remove the meat and set aside. Add the jamón Ibérico and fry for a couple of minutes until just starting to crisp. Remove and set aside. Reduce the heat to medium, add the veg to the saucepan and cook for 10 minutes until softened, adding more oil if necessary.

Place the pork back into the saucepan with the stock and the reserved marinade liquid. Bring to a boil, then turn down to a simmer. Cover and cook for 2 hours, until the cheeks are tender. Remove the lid and place the pork cheeks onto a plate or chopping board, then cook the liquor for a further 30 minutes to reduce to a coating consistency. Once reduced, check the seasoning and adjust if necessary.

Return the meat to the sauce to heat through and serve with chunks of bread.

Flamenquín with mustard mayo & chips

Serves 4

2 × 300 g (10½ oz) pork fillets, butterflied (ask your butcher to do this for you)
8 slices of serrano ham
150 g (5 oz) Andalusian melting cheese, such as Payoyo sheep's cheese, or any semi-cured Manchego, grated
sea salt and freshly ground black pepper
3 tablespoons plain (all-purpose) flour
2 free-range eggs, beaten
150 g (5 oz/1½ cups) fine dry breadcrumbs
olive oil, for frying

For the mustard mayo
2 free-range egg yolks
1 teaspoon Dijon mustard
sea salt and freshly ground black pepper
300 ml (10 fl oz/1¼ cups) light olive oil
squeeze of lemon juice, to taste

For the chips
700 g (1 lb 8½ oz) potatoes, peeled and cut into thin chips
sea salt
olive oil or vegetable oil, for deep-frying

The harder I tried to discover the origin of *flamenquín*, the more confusing it became. The name of the dish translates as 'flamenco dancer'; I'm going to say that it likely comes from Córdoba, and the most popular version contains pork fillet, serrano ham and cheese.

First, make the mustard mayo. In a small bowl, beat the egg yolks with the mustard and plenty of seasoning. Gradually whisk in the oil until you have a smooth, thick mayo. Add a little lemon juice to taste, then chill until needed.

To make the chips, place the potatoes in a saucepan of cold, salted water, bring to a boil and simmer very gently for 4–5 minutes, until tender. Drain well, spread out onto a baking tray (pan) and chill in the fridge for 1 hour.

Heat the oil in a deep saucepan to 130°C (260°F) and fry the potatoes for 7–8 minutes, until lightly golden; you may need to do this in batches. Drain well and set aside to cool.

Place the pork fillets between two sheets of cling film (plastic wrap). Using a rolling pin, gently bash the fillets so each flattens a little, trying not to break the flesh. Cut each flattened fillet in half. Lay 2 slices of serrano ham over each piece of pork, add a handful of grated cheese and roll up.

Place the flour, eggs and breadcrumbs into three separate bowls. Whisk a little seasoning into the flour. Dust each flamenquín in the flour, then dip in beaten egg and finally roll in breadcrumbs until evenly coated.

Heat around 2 cm (¾ in) oil in a frying pan over a medium heat and fry the flamenquíns for about 4–5 minutes, turning frequently, until golden brown all over and cooked through. Drain on kitchen paper and keep warm while you finish cooking the chips.

Return the saucepan of oil to the heat and bring the temperature up to 200°C (400°F). Fry the chips for a second time, until golden brown and crispy, about 2 minutes. Drain the chips on kitchen paper. Season both the chips and flamenquíns with sea salt and serve with the mustard mayo.

Lomo en manteca

Serves 6, with leftovers for
Plato de los montes (page 36)

1 kg (2 lb 3 oz) pork loin,
    thickly sliced
3 garlic cloves, bashed
large handful of fresh oregano,
    chopped
pared zest of 1 lemon
125 ml (4 fl oz/½ cup) white
    wine vinegar
1 kg (2 lb 3 oz) pork lard or
    Ibérico pork fat (ask your
    butcher for this)
2 teaspoons smoked pimentón
    de la Vera

To serve
crusty bread
fat green olives
dry sherry (such as fino)

Lomo en manteca literally means 'loin in fat', and I love it so much. In days gone by, this was a way of preserving meat for the whole year. Normally it contains few ingredients, but I do like to add one or two spices for variation – here, I use smoked pimentón de la Vera.

Place the pork loin slices in a glass or ceramic dish. Whisk together the garlic, oregano, lemon zest and vinegar with 100 ml (3½ fl oz/scant ½ cup) water and pour over the pork. Cover the dish with cling film (plastic wrap) and marinate in the fridge for 24 hours. Strain and wipe off the herbs, garlic and lemon zest.

Melt the pork fat in a heavy-based saucepan or casserole dish over a medium-low heat. Add the pork loin slices, making sure they are well covered by the melted fat. Cook over a very low heat for 2–2½ hours until very tender and cooked through, but not browned, adding the smoked pimentón for the last half an hour of cooking. Allow to cool completely in the fat (you can transfer to an earthenware pot if you prefer) and chill until the lard has hardened.

When you are ready to eat, remove the slices from the fat and thinly slice. Serve on pieces of bread, spread with some of the flavoured fat, with olives and a glass of chilled wine or sherry.

Plato de los montes

Serves 4

To me, this is the Spanish equivalent of an English breakfast – a big plate of deliciousness that will keep you going all day. It's served in *ventas*, or roadside cafés, on the mountain roads around Malága (try the road between Malága and Colmenar). In days gone by, it would have been eaten daily, but now it's more of a family breakfast treat on a Sunday.

500 g (1 lb 2 oz) potatoes, peeled and diced
2 tablespoons extra-virgin olive oil
150 g (5 oz) cooking chorizo, sliced
150 g (5 oz) morcilla, sliced
1 green (bell) pepper, deseeded and sliced
2 thick pieces of Lomo en manteca (see page 35)
4 free-range eggs

Place the potatoes in a pan of cold salted water, bring to a boil and simmer for 5 minutes, until tender. Drain well then return the potatoes to the pan over a very low heat to dry out. Set aside.

Pour the oil into a large frying pan over a medium heat. Add the chorizo and morcilla, and fry until crisp and the fat has been released, for about 2–3 minutes. Remove with a slotted spoon and keep warm.

Fry the peppers in the chorizo and morcilla fat for 3–4 minutes, until softened. Remove and set aside with the chorizo and morcilla.

Add a little more oil to the pan and fry the potatoes over a medium-high heat until golden and crisp, about 5 minutes. Push to one side and add the slices of Lomo en manteca to the pan and warm through. Remove and set aside with the meats and pepper.

Finally, fry the eggs in the remaining oil, until the whites are cooked but the yolks are still runny, or however you would prefer. Serve the crispy potatoes and Lomo en manteca with the chorizo, morcilla and peppers on individual plates with an egg on top of each portion.

Venison fillet with wild mushrooms & chestnuts

Serves 4 as a starter or light lunch

This recipe was given to me by my dear friend Vicente Taberner; Vicente and Anne own Huerta de Albalá winery in Cádiz. We've worked together to make our own wine, which has been an amazing experience, creating something unique for everyone to enjoy.

The milk in this recipe balances the strong flavour of the meat, so the taste is surprisingly delicate.

1 × 500 g (1 lb 2 oz) venison fillet
500 ml (17 fl oz/2 cups) whole (full-fat) milk
1 teaspoon black peppercorns
1 star anise
1 teaspoon juniper berries, lightly crushed
sea salt and freshly ground black pepper
olive oil, for frying
250 g (9 oz) wild mushrooms, such as ceps, chanterelles, black trumpets and saffron milk caps
2 garlic cloves, finely sliced
few sprigs of thyme, leaves picked
100 g (3½ oz) chestnuts, cooked, peeled and roughly chopped
2 tablespoons sherry vinegar
20 g (¾ oz) membrillo, diced
2–3 tablespoons chicken stock
handful of rocket (arugula) leaves
extra-virgin olive oil, for drizzling

Place the venison in a glass or ceramic dish and cover with the milk. Add the spices to the dish, cover with cling film (plastic wrap) and marinate overnight in the fridge.

The next day, remove the meat from the milk, pat dry and season all over. Heat a little oil in a large frying pan until really hot and sear the venison all over for 2 minutes on each side, until really well browned and caramelised. Allow to cool a little, then wrap tightly in cling film and chill in the fridge for 2–3 hours.

When ready to serve, pour a little more oil into a pan over a medium-high heat. Add the mushrooms, garlic and thyme and fry for 4–5 minutes, until golden. Add the chestnuts and cook for 1 minute more, then add the sherry vinegar, membrillo and stock. Cook for 2–3 minutes to reduce slightly. Remove from the heat and season well.

Unwrap the venison and slice it as finely as possible. Spoon the mushrooms onto individual plates and top with the thinly sliced venison. Scatter over the rocket, drizzle with extra-virgin olive oil and finish with sea salt and freshly ground black pepper before serving.

José's mum's pork ribs

Serves 4–6

My mother, Isabel, knows how much I love her ribs recipe, and she always wants to cook them for me when I go home to visit her. Obviously, you won't be able to try them for yourselves, but a close second is found at José Vicente, a restaurant in Aracena, where the ribs are from Cinco Jotas, a supplier of the finest Ibérico pork, and are cooked very simply, with a little bit of salt over a low heat, almost like my mum's: divine.

100 ml (3½ fl oz/scant ½ cup)
    extra-virgin olive oil
200 ml (7 fl oz/¾ cup)
    white wine
2 tablespoons dried oregano
3 garlic cloves, finely chopped
juice of 1 lemon
sea salt and freshly ground
    black pepper
1.3 kg (2 lb 13 oz) rack Ibérico
    pork ribs, or spare ribs, cut
    individually (you can ask your
    butcher to do this for you)

Combine the olive oil, wine, oregano, garlic and lemon juice in a ceramic or glass dish and season with salt and pepper. Add the ribs, cover the dish with cling film (plastic wrap) and marinate in the fridge for at least 8 hours, or preferably overnight.

Preheat the oven to 150°C (300°F/Gas 2) and take the meat out of the fridge.

Place the ribs into a large roasting tin, leaving space between each one, and pour over half of the marinade. Season with a little salt and roast for 20 minutes.

Increase the heat to 200°C (400°F/Gas 6) and cook for another 30 minutes, until caramelised and crisp, turning the ribs over occasionally, until dark and tender. A few minutes before taking the ribs out of the oven, add the rest of the marinade.

Remove from the tin and serve immediately.

Roast chicken with orange, cumin & apricot rice

Serves 6

This is a classic one pot dish that I often make at home. Every part of the meal is comforting and delicious, but the truly heavenly bit is the crispy anchovy-flavoured chicken skin.

2 large garlic cloves, peeled
2 tablespoons extra-virgin olive oil, plus extra for frying
6 salted anchovies in extra-virgin olive oil
1 large free-range chicken (1.8 kg/3 lb 15 oz)
sea salt and freshly ground black pepper
2 banana shallots (eschalions), finely sliced
½ tablespoon cumin seeds
½ tablespoon sweet smoked pimentón de la Vera
1 tablespoon hot smoked pimentón de la Vera
500 g (1 lb 2 oz) Calasparra rice or another short-grain rice, soaked for 10 minutes in cold water and drained
zest and juice of ½ orange
100 g (3½ oz) dried apricots, chopped
1 bay leaf
1 sprig of rosemary
1 litre (34 fl oz/4 cups) chicken stock
small bunch of flat-leaf parsley, roughly chopped

Preheat the oven to 200°C (400°F/Gas 6).

In small food processor or heavy pestle and mortar, blend the garlic cloves with the olive oil and half of the anchovies to a rough paste.

Carefully loosen the skin from the breasts of the chicken and rub the garlic and anchovy mixture underneath the skin. Season well with salt. Place the chicken in a deep, lidded casserole dish and roast, uncovered, for 35 minutes, until the skin is golden.

Meanwhile, add a little oil to a saucepan and fry the shallots with the rest of the anchovies and a pinch of salt over a medium heat for 5 minutes, or until softened. Add the cumin seeds and both types of pimentón and fry for 1–2 minutes, until fragrant. Mix in the rice, orange zest and juice and dried apricots. Add the bay leaf, rosemary and the chicken stock, bring to a boil, then remove from the heat and set aside.

Remove the casserole dish from the oven, carefully lift out the chicken and place on a chopping board. Add the rice and stock mixture to the dish and place the chicken back on top. Reduce the oven to 180°C (350°F/Gas 4) and roast, covered, for 1 hour. At this point, check to see if the rice is cooked. If needed, add a little more stock and cook for a further 10 minutes.

Remove the casserole dish from the oven and lift the chicken back onto the chopping board, tipping it over the dish first so that any juices run back into the rice. Leave the chicken to rest for 5–10 minutes, loosely covered with foil. Taste the rice, season and stir through the parsley. Place the lid back on the dish to keep warm as you carve the chicken. Dish up onto warm plates with the rice.

Lamb sweetbreads with chilli & rosemary

Serves 2

I love to cook sweetbreads, especially ones from young lambs as they are so tender and delicate in flavour. There are many different ways to prepare them – it's hard to beat battered and deep fried with some lemon allioli, or simply grilled, but I'd say this recipe just about pips both methods to the post.

300 g (10½ oz) lamb sweetbreads, soaked in cold water for 2 hours
olive oil, for frying
2 garlic cloves, finely sliced
good pinch of chilli flakes
2 sprigs of rosemary, leaves stripped
2 tablespoons plain (all-purpose) flour
sea salt and freshly ground black pepper
splash of fino sherry
4 tablespoons chicken stock
1 tablespoon finely chopped flat-leaf parsley
4 slices of crusty bread, toasted
extra-virgin olive oil, for drizzling

Bring a saucepan of water to a boil. Add the sweetbreads and blanch for 1 minute, then drain and cool quickly under cold water. Peel off and discard the outer skin and pat them dry with kitchen paper. Set aside.

Pour a little oil into a frying pan over a low heat. Add the garlic, chilli and rosemary and allow to warm gently.

Place the flour in a small bowl with a little seasoning and dust the sweetbreads in the flour. Increase the heat to medium-high, add the sweetbreads to the pan and sear for 3–4 minutes each side, until browned. Remove the sweetbreads from the pan and set aside.

Add a splash of sherry to the frying pan and cook for 30 seconds, scraping up all the lovely sticky bits. Add the stock and bring to a bubble. Stir in the parsley.

Serve immediately, with the sweetbreads placed on the toast, the sauce spooned over the top, and a good drizzle of extra-virgin olive oil to finish.

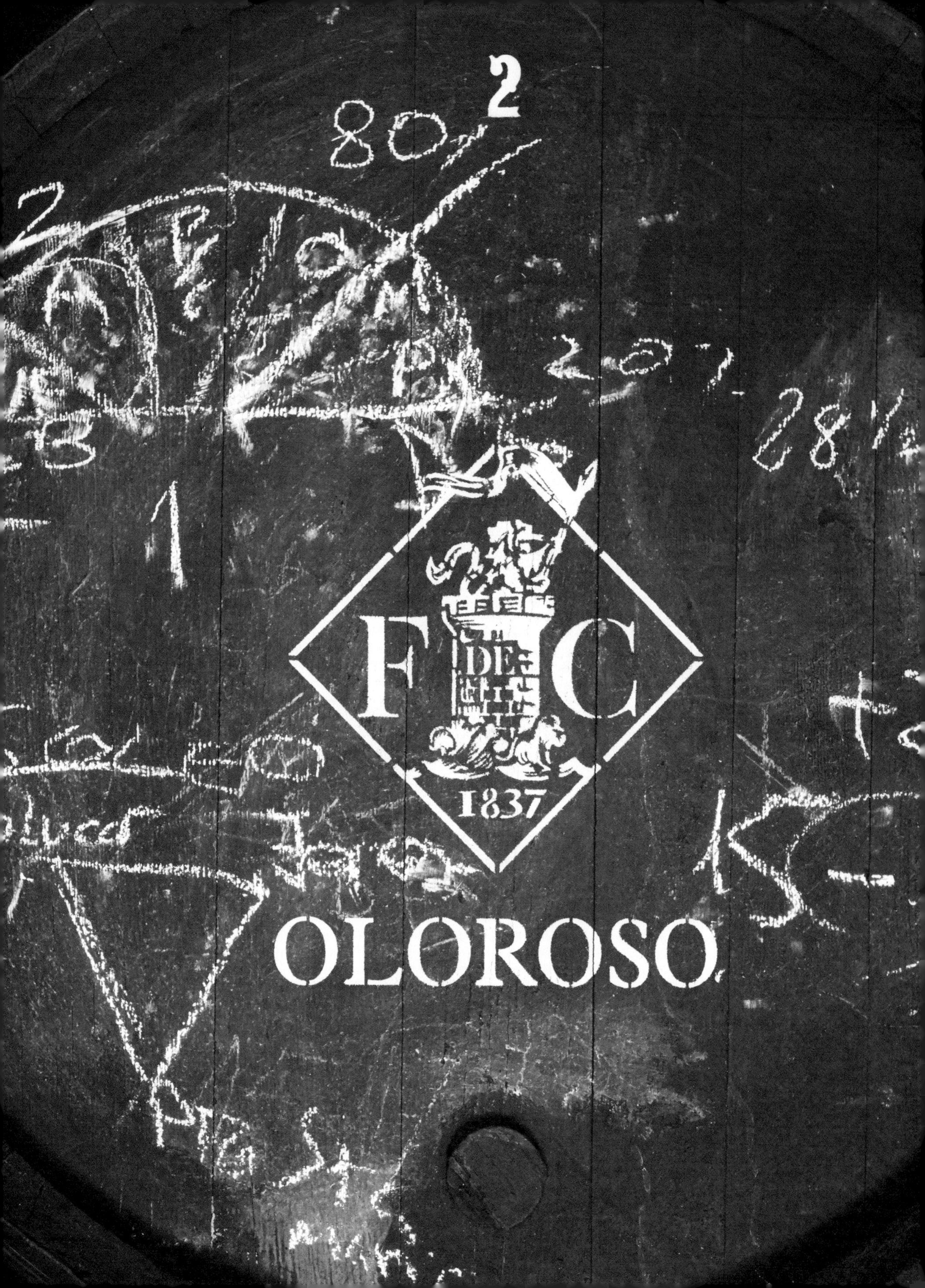
2
F C
1837
OLOROSO

Caldereta del cordero

Serves 4–6

The word *caldereta* comes from *caldero*, which is a big pan normally used on an open fire.

Stews are very popular all over Spain, and can be made with meat, like this version with lamb, or fish. In the Balearic Islands, they make a *caldereta* with lobster, which is my absolute favourite.

sea salt and freshly ground
    black pepper
1.2 kg (2 lb 10 oz) lamb shoulder,
    roughly diced
olive oil, for frying
1 large onion, finely chopped
3 garlic cloves, crushed
2 red (bell) peppers, deseeded
    and finely sliced
2 bay leaves
2 sprigs of rosemary
3 sprigs of thyme
200 ml (7 fl oz/¾ cup) red wine
600 g (1 lb 5 oz) fresh tomatoes,
    chopped
1 tablespoon tomato purée
500 ml (17 fl oz/2 cups) chicken
    stock

For the picada
olive oil, for frying
50 g (2 oz) slice stale bread,
    broken into pieces
50 g (2 oz) blanched almonds
3 dried choricero peppers,
    soaked in boiling water for
    10 minutes

To serve
crusty bread or boiled potatoes

Season the lamb, then add a little oil to a saucepan over a medium-high heat and fry the lamb until well browned all over; you'll need to do this in batches. Remove from the saucepan and set aside.

Add more oil to the saucepan, reduce to a medium heat and add the onion. Fry for 10 minutes, until golden and softened, then add the garlic, peppers and herbs. Cook until the peppers start to soften, around 5 minutes. Pour in the red wine and let bubble for 1 minute to reduce a little. Return the lamb to the pot and add the tomatoes, tomato purée and chicken stock. Bring to the boil then reduce to a simmer and slowly cook over a low heat for 2–2½ hours, until the meat is really tender.

While the lamb is cooking, make the picada. Heat a little oil in a heavy-based saucepan over a medium heat and fry the bread and almonds for a minute or two, until lightly toasted, then tip into a pestle and mortar or a small food processor and crush with the soaked choricero peppers and a little of their soaking water to make a paste.

Stir in the picada of peppers, bread and almonds and cook for 4–5 minutes to thicken. Serve immediately with crusty bread or potatoes.

Moorish wild boar stew

Serves 4

Boar is a fantastic meat. The taste is unparalleled because the boar roam around the woodland, eating flora and fauna – very happy pigs. You can find it easily online, or ask your local butcher. I can't claim that this is a specifically a Spanish recipe, but it is very popular in Andalusia.

1 kg (2 lb 3 oz) wild boar, cut into chunks
250 ml (8½ fl oz/1 cup) Palo Cortado sherry
olive oil, for frying
2 large onions, finely chopped
4 garlic cloves, crushed
2 teaspoons cumin seeds
1 teaspoon ground coriander
pinch of ground cinnamon
150 g (5 oz) Muscatel raisins, or large sultanas
30 g (1 oz) 100% cacao chocolate
zest and juice of 1 orange
1 litre (34 fl oz/4 cups) chicken stock
sea salt and freshly ground black pepper

For the couscous
300 g (10½ oz/1¾ cups) couscous
450 ml (15 fl oz/scant 2 cups) hot chicken stock
extra-virgin olive oil, for drizzling
juice of 1 lemon
sea salt and freshly ground black pepper
large bunch of flat-leaf parsley, leaves chopped

Place the boar in a glass or ceramic dish. Pour over the sherry, cover with cling film (plastic wrap) and marinate in the fridge for at least 8 hours, or preferably overnight.

Add some oil to a large lidded casserole dish over a medium heat. Fry the onions gently for 10 minutes, until soft and slightly golden. Add the garlic and cumin seeds and fry for a minute more.

Drain and reserve the sherry from the meat. Pat it dry with kitchen paper and add to the pan. Fry until well browned, around 5 minutes.

Pour the sherry into the pan with the coriander and cinnamon and bubble for a minute or two before adding the raisins, chocolate, orange zest and juice and the stock. Season well and bring to a boil, then reduce to a simmer and leave to cook, covered, stirring occasionally, for 2½ hours. Partially uncover, leaving the lid slightly ajar, then cook for a further 40 minutes until the meat is tender and the sauce is reduced and thickened.

Put the couscous into a shallow serving bowl. Pour over the hot stock and then cover with cling film and leave to stand for 5–6 minutes, until all the liquid has been absorbed. Fluff it up with a fork and drizzle over a generous amount of extra-virgin olive oil, followed by the lemon juice. Season to taste and stir through the parsley. Serve immediately with the wild boar stew.

Pringás

Serves 6

You cannot beat *pringás* and a coffee for breakfast, and one of the best places to have it is at Las Columnas on Bodega Santa Cruz in Seville. Visit once, and I guarantee you'll be back again – the staff are great, and you are bound to have a laugh with them.

100 g (3½ oz) beef dripping
    or lard
1 large onion, roughly chopped
1 celery stalk, chopped
1 carrot, chopped
1 teaspoon black peppercorns
2 bay leaves
6 fat chicken wings
200 g (7 oz) pork belly strips
1 pig's trotter
150 g (5 oz) cooking chorizo,
    skin split
150 g (5 oz) beef shin
100 g (3½ oz) morcilla,
    crumbled
2 teaspoons hot smoked
    pimentón de la Vera
1 teaspoon sweet smoked
    pimentón de la Vera
sea salt and freshly ground
    black pepper

To serve
crusty bread, sliced and
    toasted

Melt 1 tablespoon of the dripping or lard in a large casserole dish or heavy-based saucepan over a medium heat. Add the onion, celery and carrot and fry for 10 minutes, until slightly softened, then add the peppercorns, bay leaves and meat.

Cover with water and bring to a boil, then reduce the heat and very gently simmer for 2 ½–3 hours, until the meat is falling apart. Remove the meat and vegetables and discard the peppercorns and bay leaves. Leave to cool.

Shred all the meat into a bowl, discarding the skin and bones.

Melt the rest of the dripping or lard in a frying pan over a low-medium heat and add both types of pimentón, the meat and vegetables. Mix together, mashing it up roughly. Season to taste and serve warm, or at room temperature, spread over the toast.

Tenderloin with pears & hazelnuts

Serves 4–6

The first time I cooked Ibérico pork in London was around 2001, when I was working with the chef David Eyre. When I described it to him, he thought I was crazy – medium rare pork?! Once he tried it though, we put it on the menu and it became a favourite at the restaurant. If you are not using Ibérico pork, make sure to cook the fillet for 10–15 minutes longer until it is cooked all the way through. I first created this recipe for a collaboration with my friends at Cinco Jotas. Whenever I meet my dear friend Maria Castro, I always have to cook this for her.

1 × 800 g (1 lb 12 oz) pork tenderloin, preferably Ibérico
150 ml (5 fl oz/⅔ cup) extra-virgin olive oil, plus extra for frying
sea salt and freshly ground black pepper
50 ml (2 fl oz/¼ cup) sherry vinegar
3–4 sprigs of fresh thyme
½ tablespoon ground cumin
1 teaspoon sweet smoked pimentón de la Vera
1 large garlic clove, very finely chopped

For the pears & hazelnuts
3 ripe comice pears, peeled, cored and finely sliced
juice of 1 lemon
50 g (2 oz) skin-on hazelnuts, toasted
fresh thyme leaves, to garnish

Place a frying pan, large enough to fit the pork loin, over a high heat. Rub the loin in a little oil and season well. Sear the loin on all sides, around 4–5 minutes, until caramelised, then lift out of the pan and place in a deep glass or ceramic dish.

Mix the oil, vinegar, thyme, cumin, pimentón and garlic together in a small bowl, then pour over the pork. Cover and marinate in the fridge for at least 8 hours.

Bring the pork out of the fridge 30 minutes before serving, so it comes to room temperature.

When almost ready to serve, gently toss the pears in a bowl with the lemon juice.

Remove the pork from the marinade, reserving the liquid, and cut into 1 cm (½ in) slices. Place the slices onto individual plates or a sharing platter with the pear and toasted hazelnuts and spoon over the reserved pork marinade. Top with fresh thyme leaves and serve.

Fried rabbit

Serves 4

In La Janda, an area north of Cádiz, you can find *gazapo*, which is a small rabbit that's really tender and delicious, especially when fried. Persimmons grow all over Andalusia and are known as *kaqui*; the persimmon salsa provides a soft contrast to the crispy rabbit, and brings some moisture to a dish that can otherwise be a bit dry.

2 small rabbits, preferably wild, jointed
3 teaspoons ground cumin
3 teaspoons ground coriander
pinch of ground cinnamon
1 star anise
3 tablespoons extra-virgin olive oil
50 ml (2 fl oz/¼ cup) sherry or white wine vinegar
sea salt and freshly ground black pepper
2 free-range eggs, beaten
100 g (3½ oz/¾ cup) plain (all-purpose) flour
2 teaspoons hot smoked pimentón de la Vera

For the persimmon salsa
4 persimmons, peeled and diced
2 vine-ripened tomatoes, diced
1 red chilli, deseeded and finely chopped
4 spring onions, finely sliced
handful of mint leaves, shredded
handful of coriander (cilantro) leaves, chopped
good squeeze of lime juice
extra-virgin olive oil, for drizzling
sea salt and freshly ground black pepper

Place the rabbits in a glass or ceramic dish with 1 teaspoon each of cumin and coriander, the cinnamon, star anise, the olive oil and the vinegar. Season, cover with cling film (plastic wrap) and marinate in the fridge for at least 1 hour, or up to overnight. If leaving overnight, add the seasoning in the morning.

Just before you are ready to cook the rabbit, mix all the ingredients for the salsa together in a small bowl with some seasoning. Set aside.

Preheat the oven to 160°C (320°F/Gas 3).

Pour the beaten eggs into a shallow bowl. Mix the flour with plenty of seasoning and the rest of the ground cumin, coriander and the pimentón in a separate bowl.

Half-fill a deep saucepan with oil and heat to 180°C (350°F) – or until a cube of bread browns in about 30 seconds.

Remove the rabbit from the marinade and dip the pieces in beaten egg and then coat in flour. Repeat the process so that you have a good, thick coating.

Working in batches, lower the rabbit pieces into the hot oil and cook for 10–12 minutes until golden, crisp and cooked through. Transfer to a baking tray (pan) and pop into the preheated oven to stay warm while you cook the rest.

Once all the rabbit pieces are cooked, pile onto a platter and serve with the persimmon salsa.

Perdiz encebollada

Serves 4

Las Tinajas is a restaurant in Granada and a veritable institution. The walls are full of photos of famous people who have visited since 1971, so it's as old as me! It's now run by José and his sister Silvia, but it was their father, also called José, who shared this recipe with me.

4 partridges
2 onions, finely sliced
2 carrots, finely chopped
1 leek, finely sliced
250 ml (8½ fl oz/1 cup) white
    wine
2 bay leaves
3–4 sprigs of thyme
sea salt and freshly ground
    black pepper
olive oil, for frying
5 garlic cloves, finely sliced
1 teaspoon black peppercorns
600 ml (20 fl oz/2½ cups)
    chicken stock

To serve
crusty bread

Place the partridges in a glass or ceramic dish with the onions, carrots and leek, pour over the wine and add the herbs. Cover with cling film (plastic wrap) and marinate in the fridge for 24 hours.

Remove the partridges from the marinade, strain the vegetables from the wine and reserve both.

Heat a little oil in a lidded casserole dish (large enough to fit the birds) over a medium-high heat. Season the meat with salt and brown all over. Set aside.

Heat a little more oil in the casserole dish, add the garlic and cook for 30 seconds, until fragrant. Add the reserved vegetables and cook for 10 minutes, until softened. Pour in the reserved wine and bubble for 1–2 minutes. Return the partridges to the casserole dish and add the black peppercorns and stock. Bring to a boil then reduce to a simmer. Cover and cook over a low heat for 1 hour, then partially uncover by leaving the lid slightly ajar and cook for a further 30–40 minutes, until the partridges are really tender and the sauce has reduced.

Remove the partridges from the pan, joint the legs, remove the breasts and slice, then serve with the sauce, with crusty bread on the side.

Andalusia has been influenced by many cultures, and thanks to this, there are a lot of different ways in which people prepare fish here. One of the most delicious is *salazón*, or salt fish, introduced by the Phoenicians. Originally this was a traded commodity, as well as a way to preserve the catch, maintaining its popularity all throughout the Roman period, when Almuñécar, a town on Granada's coast, and Cádiz were two of the most important ports in the world. The style of cooking endures to this day.

Arabic culture, of course, also changed the way fish were caught and prepared. For example, the ancient technique used to catch tuna off the Cádiz coast, known as *la almadraba*, takes advantage of the tuna's migratory path, and is unique to this part of Spain.

But whatever the heritage of the cooking methods, to my mind, there is nothing better than a cold sherry with white prawns (shrimp) from Huelva or red from Almería, and *pescaíto frito* to pair with a sea view.

Prawns baked in salt with mango, chilli & coriander salsa

Serves 4

I always use Andalusian mangoes when I make this dish, and chilli perfectly balances the sweetness of the fruit and shellfish. *Carabineros* are very popular in Catalonia and, in my opinion, the best ones come from Palamos. This type of prawn (shrimp) has a very intense flavour and vivid red colour that only intensifies once cooked.

3 mangoes, peeled, stone
    removed and cubed
1 red chilli, deseeded and finely
    chopped
sea salt and freshly ground
    black pepper
juice of 1 lime
extra-virgin olive oil, for drizzling
zest and juice of ½ orange
1 small bunch of coriander
    (cilantro), chopped

For the prawns
850 g (1 lb 14 oz) coarse
    sea salt
2 egg whites, lightly beaten
    until frothy
1 teaspoon coriander seeds
zest of 1 orange
12 raw carabineros or large king
    prawns (shrimp)
extra-virgin olive oil,
    for brushing

Preheat the oven to 200°C (400°F/Gas 6).

In a medium bowl, mix the mango with the red chillies and a pinch of salt and pepper. Squeeze over the lime juice, orange zest and juice and a drizzle of olive oil. Toss with the coriander and set aside while you cook the prawns.

Mix the salt, egg whites, coriander seeds and orange zest together in a medium bowl and tip half into a baking dish. Place the prawns on top of the salt, brush them with a little oil, then completely bury them with the rest of the salt. Bake in the oven for 8–10 minutes, until just cooked.

Remove the prawns from the oven and gently uncover them to check they are all cooked – if not, put them back in the oven for a minute or two.

Scrape off the salt and serve the salsa with the hot prawns, or let them cool to room temperature, then serve.

Sopa bullabesa de Almería

Serves 4–6

I think the name of this dish came from the soup *bouillabaisse de Marsella*, and, just like its namesake, it is a delicious fish stew. Feel free to adapt or play around with using different fish and seafood, as this depends entirely on the season and what you can get from your fishmonger – my only advice is fresh and seasonal will always make a superior soup. In some areas, the restaurants added allioli or mayonnaise, but I prefer it without.

olive oil, for frying
1 onion, finely chopped
1 bulb of fennel, finely chopped, fronds reserved
2 teaspoons smoked pimentón de la Vera
pinch of saffron, soaked in 2 tablespoons boiling water
200 ml (2 fl oz/¾ cup) white wine
50 ml (2 fl oz/¼ cup) Pernod or other anise liqueur
300 g (10½ oz) ripe tomatoes, skinned and chopped
zest and juice of ½ orange
200 ml (2 fl oz/¾ cup) shellfish or fish stock
sea salt and freshly ground black pepper
400 g (14 oz) monkfish, cut into chunks
400 g (14 oz) clams, cleaned
500 g (1 lb 2 oz) raw prawns (shrimp), shell on

To serve
crusty bread

Pour the olive oil into a large frying pan over a medium heat and gently cook the onion and fennel for 15 minutes, until softened. Add the pimentón and saffron with its soaking liquid, then pour in the wine and Pernod and bubble for 1–2 minutes.

Add the tomatoes, orange zest, juice and stock. Check the seasoning and bring to a simmer.

Add the monkfish to the pan and cook for 3–4 minutes, then add the clams and prawns and cook for a further 2–3 minutes, until the prawns are pink and the clams are open (discard any clams that have not opened).

Scatter with the reserved fennel fronds and serve with crusty bread.

Fried anchovies with allioli

Serves 4

On a hot day on the Andalusian coast, *pescado frito*, or fried fish, is tremendously popular. There are often many different kinds of fish on the plate, from little red mullet and slip sole to baby squid. But, in my opinion, you just can't beat a big plate of fried anchovies, with some lemon and allioli – add a cold beer and it's heaven.

800 g (1 lb 12 oz) fresh
    anchovies
55 g (2 oz/½ cup) plain
    (all-purpose) flour
2 teaspoons cornflour
    (cornstarch)
sea salt and freshly ground
    black pepper
1 litre (34 fl oz/4 cups) light
    olive oil
1 lemon, quartered

For the allioli
2 free-range egg yolks
1 garlic clove, finely crushed
sea salt and freshly ground
    black pepper
250–300 ml (8½–10 fl oz/
    1–1¼ cups) light olive oil
squeeze of lemon juice

First, clean the anchovies. Wash well, then remove the heads, slit the bellies and take out the insides. Then, with a sharp knife and fingers, pull out the bones. This will leave you with butterflied fillets. Alternatively, you can ask your fishmonger to do this for you.

To make the allioli, mix the egg yolks and garlic together with salt and pepper, then gradually whisk in the olive oil until you have a thick mayonnaise. Season with lemon juice and add a little more salt or pepper to taste.

Mix the flours with some seasoning in a shallow bowl. Heat the oil in a deep saucepan to 180°C (350°F) – or until a cube of bread browns in about 20 seconds. Dust the fish in the seasoned flour and fry for 1–2 minutes, until golden and just cooked. Drain on kitchen paper and sprinkle with sea salt.

Serve the fried fish immediately with the allioli to dip them in and lemon wedges to squeeze over.

Espeto

Serves 4

During my research travelling all along the Cádiz coastline, people were excited to tell me about the origins of *espeto*, a very simple but famous dish. A few small, fresh sardines skewered and grilled over wood, it came from a humble neighbourhood called El Palo in Málaga, where fishing was the most common source of income. The fishermen took the initiative to develop the area and started selling the fresh fish in beach bars, or *merenderos*, as they are called in Málaga.

After trying more versions than I can remember, I cooked *espeto* in Sanlucar de Barrameda at Chiringuito La Orilla. Baldomero, the chef at the time, cooked 110–120 *espetos* a day in summer. Baldomero used olive and oak wood for the fire, and just splashed water on his hands to turn the skewer and avoid being burned. The sardines are cooked as they are with no extra oil, and you can tell they are done when the eyes turn white. This absolutely the healthiest way to eat fish.

12 medium sardines, gutted
sea salt and freshly ground
    black pepper
few sprigs of rosemary
    or thyme
extra-virgin olive oil, plus extra
    for drizzling
2–3 baby gem lettuce, halved
bunch of spring onions
    (scallions)
juice of 1 lemon
large handful of mixed flat-leaf
    parsley, chervil (optional) and
    chives, chopped

Light a charcoal barbecue and add some kindling to get it nice and hot and full of flames. Spear the sardines onto large metal or wooden skewers (if using wooden skewers, soak them in warm water for 30 minutes before using), and season with sea salt.

Throw a few sprigs of rosemary or thyme onto the coals to produce some lovely aromatic smoke, then put the fish onto the barbecue and cook for 3–4 minutes on each side, until the skin is blackened.

Lightly oil the baby gem lettuce halves and spring onions and char on the barbecue next to the fish for 2–3 minutes, until tender. Put the lettuce and spring onions into a bowl and squeeze over the lemon juice, lots of extra-virgin olive oil and plenty of seasoning. Stir in the chopped herbs and serve with the fish.

Beer-battered hake

Serves 4

It's a bit of a mystery as to where fish and chips originally came from, however some believe that it arrived in the UK hundreds of years ago, brought by the Jewish from the Iberian peninsula.

In Seville there is a very popular tapa called *pavia*, which is very similar to a fish finger! And of course, fish and chips.

I always eat pavia at Casa Morales in Seville, a restaurant that's been running since 1850 – the family arrived in Andalusia to sell wine from Valdepeñas in Castilla La Mancha, and have been there ever since. You can substitute the hake with cod, if wished.

70 g (2½ oz/⅔ cup) cornflour (cornstarch)
70 g (2½ oz/½ cup) plain (all-purpose) flour
sea salt and freshly ground black pepper
2 litres (68 fl oz/8 cups) sunflower oil
800 ml (27 fl oz/3½ cups) pilsner lager
8 × 100 g (3½ oz) fillets of hake (or cod)

Mix the flours in a medium bowl, season well and set aside.

Heat the oil in a deep saucepan to 180°C (350°F) – or until a cube of bread browns in about 20 seconds.

Whisk the beer into the flours until well incorporated. Place the fish into the batter, turning until well coated.

Lower the batter-coated fish into the oil with heatproof tongs. Hold under the oil for a few seconds, then release into the oil. Cook for 3 minutes, or until the batter is golden and crisp. Remove with the tongs or a slotted spoon and place on to kitchen paper to drain any excess oil. Depending on the size of your pan, you might have to cook the fish in batches; if so, keep the cooked pieces warm in a low oven while you fry the rest.

Serve with cold beer and plenty of fries!

"FRESCAS"

5.99 €

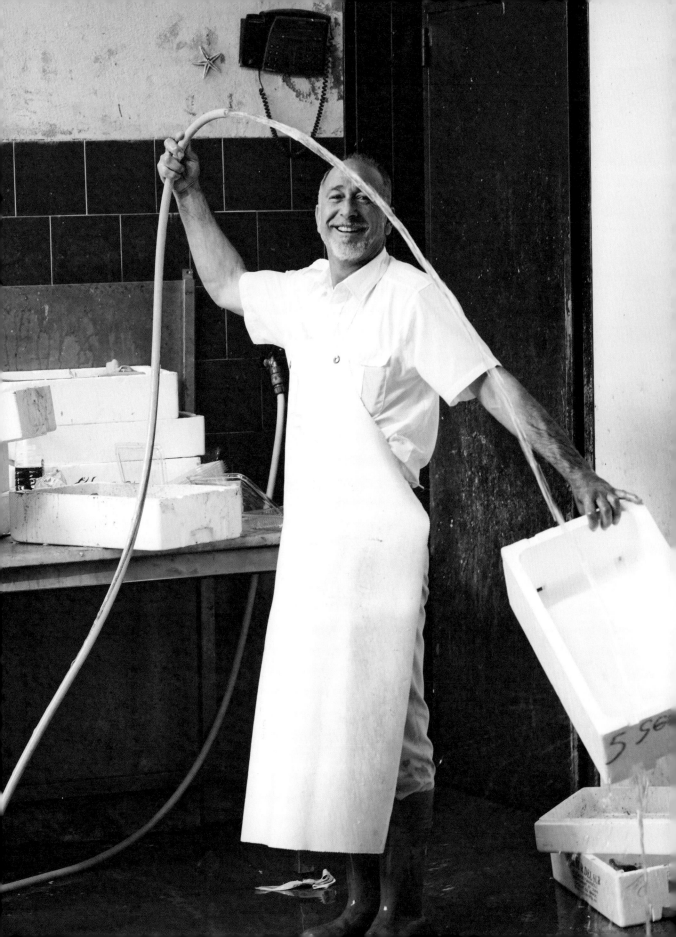

Fideos con caballa

Serves 4

This is a very popular recipe from Cádiz and San Fernando, and was traditionally eaten by fisherman. Using fish bones to make the stock, this isn't a complicated dish, but it's packed with flavour. The acidity and the sweetness from the tomatoes, onions and garlic are great levellers for the oily mackerel.

sea salt and freshly ground black pepper
2 bay leaves
4 mackerel fillets, cleaned and pin-boned, head and tail reserved
200 g (7 oz) fideos (short vermicelli pasta)
olive oil, for frying
1 large onion, finely chopped
3 ripe tomatoes, peeled and finely chopped
100 ml (3½ fl oz/scant ½ cup) white wine
3 garlic cloves, finely chopped

Fill a saucepan or shallow casserole dish with water and add a pinch of salt and the bay leaves. Add the mackerel head and tail and bring to a boil. Reduce the heat and simmer for 10 minutes. Strain the stock into a jug and discard the bay leaves, head and tail.

Pour a little olive oil into a frying pan over a medium heat and cook the onions and tomatoes in the wine for 10 minutes, or until softened. Add the garlic and fry for a further 1 minute. Ladle in the mackerel stock, bring to a boil and add the fideos. Cook for 4 minutes, or until the pasta is al dente.

Season the mackerel fillets with a little salt. Pour a little olive oil into a frying pan over a medium heat and sear the fish, skin-side down, for 2–3 minutes, until golden and almost cooked, then flip over and cook the flesh side for 30 seconds.

Divide the fideos between four pasta bowls and top with the crispy-skinned mackerel to serve.

Tuna with onions & tomatoes

Serves 4 as a tapas

Andalusia is very lucky as tuna can be caught off its shores and is often cooked fresh – in the rest of the country, it's not particularly common, and so is limited to tinned tuna and a salted variety called *mojama* (see page 114). That might sound a bit unusual, but we love it!

Two of my favourite places to eat tuna in Andalusia are Restaurante Antonio, Zahara de los Atunes, a little south of Cádiz, which has the most incredible views – and sound – of the sea, and El Campero in Barbate, where they serve every part of the tuna. Just incredible.

75–100 ml (2½–3½ fl oz/ ⅓–scant ½ cup) extra-virgin olive oil, plus extra to serve
4 large onions, finely sliced
1 bay leaf
3 very ripe tomatoes
few sprigs of fresh oregano, leaves stripped
300 g (10½ oz) sushi-grade tuna

Heat the oil in a heavy-based pan over a very low heat and fry the onion and bay leaf for 45 minutes, until extremely soft and caramelised. Set aside.

Score a cross in the base of each tomato. Place in a bowl and cover in just-boiled water. Leave for 30 seconds, remove and plunge into cold water. Peel the skins, and roughly chop the flesh. Tip into a clean bowl and set aside.

When almost ready to serve, add the tomatoes and oregano to the onions to briefly warm through, about 2–3 minutes.

Rub the tuna with oil and season well. Place a frying pan over a very high heat, until the pan is very hot, then add the tuna and sear very quickly – 1 minute on each side – so that it caramelises, but doesn't cook all the way through. The rarer the better. Remove from the pan and thinly slice into 1 cm (½ in) pieces.

Divide the onions and tomatoes between individual plates, top with the tuna slices and serve.

Papas con choco

Serves 4

Although this is served all over Andalusia, it is famously from Cádiz, where *choco* means cuttlefish. When I was researching this recipe, I discovered it was one of the oldest from the city; supposedly it came about when returning conquerors brought potatoes from America. It didn't go down so well in the royal courts, but potatoes were easily cultivated and filling, so became the base of most meals for the poor.

sea salt and freshly ground
  black pepper
2 cuttlefish, 1 kg (2 lb 3 oz),
  cleaned and sliced into 3 cm
  (1¼ in) lengths, tentacles
  reserved
olive oil, for frying
1 onion, finely sliced
2 garlic cloves, peeled and
  bashed
1 teaspoon sweet smoked
  pimentón de la Vera
1 bay leaf
2 sprigs of rosemary
400 g (14 oz) tin chopped
  tomatoes
pinch of saffron
2 litres (68 fl oz/8 cups) fish,
  chicken or vegetable stock
1 kg (2 lb 3 oz) charlotte or other
  waxy potatoes
handful of flat-leaf parsley
  leaves, roughly chopped

Season the cuttlefish. Pour a little olive oil into a heavy-based, lidded saucepan or lidded casserole dish over a high heat and fry the cuttlefish strips and tentacles for 2–3 minutes, until golden. Remove from the pan and set aside.

Add a little more oil to the saucepan and turn the heat down to medium. Fry the onion and garlic with a pinch of salt for 10 minutes, until soft. Add the smoked pimentón, herbs, chopped tomatoes and saffron and simmer for 5 minutes. Pour half of the stock into the saucepan, add the cuttlefish and bring to a boil. Simmer, covered, for 1 hour, until the fish is tender, adding a little more stock or boiled water if it's looking dry.

Meanwhile, peel the potatoes and, using a small knife, break each one into 2 cm (1¼ in) pieces so they have rough edges.

Add the potatoes to the saucepan with the remaining stock and bring to a boil. Turn down to a simmer and cook for 15 minutes, or until the potatoes are tender.

Sprinkle with plenty of parsley and serve.

Clams with chorizo

Serves 4

I love clams, whether served with jamón or just on their own with a splash of sherry or white wine. I always thought that chorizo would overpower the delicate sweetness of the clams, but to my delight, I was wrong – this is a must-try. The crispy chorizo adds a lovely texture and the smoky flavour from the pimentón de la Vera is a perfect match for fino sherry.

1 kg (2 lb 3 oz) clams
75 g (2½ oz) chorizo picante, chopped into 1 cm (½ in) cubes
1 tablespoon extra-virgin olive oil
1 small onion, finely chopped
1 garlic clove, finely chopped
large sprig of thyme
100 ml (3½ fl oz/scant ½ cup) fino sherry

To serve
crusty bread

Place the clams in a bowl under cold running water for 5 minutes. Discard any that won't close.

In a lidded saucepan over a high heat, cook the chorizo in a little olive oil for 6 minutes, until caramelised. Using a slotted spoon, remove the chorizo from the pan and place in a bowl.

Add the onion, garlic and thyme sprig to the chorizo fat in the pan and fry for 10 minutes, or until softened. Increase the heat, add the clams and chorizo back to the pan, pour in the sherry, then cover with a lid. Cook for 3 minutes, or until all the clams have steamed open, discarding any clams that haven't.

Tip into a large bowl and serve with crusty bread to mop up the juices.

Albóndigas de Semana Santa

Serves 4–6

This dish is mostly eaten at Easter; cod is very popular in Spain, although the majority comes from the stunning waters of Norway. I recently went fishing there and had the most wonderful time – I even caught 10 kg (22 lbs) of fish!

salt cod skin (see below)
150 g (5 oz) dried chickpeas (garbanzo beans), soaked overnight in cold water
150 g (5 oz) dried white beans, soaked overnight in cold water
1 garlic bulb, cloves peeled
1 bay leaf
1 small leek, cut into pieces
2 tablespoons extra-virgin olive oil
1 onion, finely chopped
1 teaspoon sweet smoked pimentón de la Vera
sea salt and freshly ground black pepper
4 eggs
2 large handfuls of spinach

For the meatballs
250 g (9 oz) salt cod, soaked for 24–48 hours in cold water, drained and skin removed and reserved
250 g (9 oz) stale bread, crusts removed
150–200 ml (5–7 fl oz/½–¾ cup) whole (full-fat) milk
large sprig of flat-leaf parsley, finely chopped
freshly ground black pepper
olive oil, for frying

Put the salt cod skin into a large saucepan with the chickpeas and white beans. Add all but 3 of the garlic cloves, the bay leaf, leek and 1 litre (34 fl oz/4 cups) cold water. Bring to a boil then simmer gently for 1½ hours, adding 750 ml (25¼ fl oz/3 cups) more water about halfway through, until the beans and chickpeas are tender. Remove and discard the fish skin, bay leaf, garlic and leek.

Pour the oil into a frying pan over a medium heat and gently cook the onion and pimentón for 10 minutes, until softened.

In a small food processor or with a hand blender, whizz the onion and a little of the stock until smooth. Transfer this mixture to the saucepan and season well.

Cook the eggs in boiling water for 6–8 minutes. Run under water to cool, then peel and quarter.

To make the meatballs, soak the bread in the milk for 2 minutes, until soft. Scoop into a large bowl. Crumble the salt cod over the bread and mix until incorporated. Finely chop the remaining garlic cloves and add to the bowl with the parsley, season with pepper and mix well. Shape into 18–20 ping-pong-sized balls.

Heat a 4 cm (2½ in) depth of oil in a frying pan to 180°C (350°F) – or until a cube of bread browns in about 20 seconds – and fry the balls until golden all over, 2–3 minutes. Once they are all browned, add them to the saucepan of chickpeas and beans with the spinach and simmer for 5–10 minutes.

Spoon the soup into individual bowls and top with the egg quarters and plenty of cracked black pepper before serving.

Smoked sardines with salmorejo

Serves 6

Salmorejo is thick, cold tomato soup that Andalusian people normally eat as a starter during summer when it's extremely hot. The dish is originally from Córdoba, where in August the temperature can easily reach 42°C (107°F). Here, I serve it with smoked sardines, as we did at Pizarro, where it was a big success, but you could add fruit such as melon or grapes to make it even fresher, if you prefer.

12 small or 6 large sardines, gutted and bones removed
handful of mild-flavoured wood chips or sawdust
2 sprigs of rosemary
2 heads of lavender
1 tablespoon fruit vinegar (raspberry, muscatel or apple are good)

For the salmorejo
800 g (1 lb 12 oz) really ripe tomatoes, cored and roughly chopped
200 g (7 oz) stale bread (ciabatta, bread roll, rustic loaf), torn
2 garlic cloves, crushed
2 teaspoons sherry vinegar
75 ml (2½ fl oz/⅓ cup) extra-virgin olive oil
sea salt and freshly ground black pepper

For the lemon thyme croutons
100 g (3½ oz) stale bread, cubed
olive oil, for frying
3–4 sprigs of lemon thyme
sea salt

To serve
3 free-range eggs
extra-virgin olive oil, for drizzling

First, clean the sardines. Wash well, then remove the heads, slit the bellies and take out the insides. Then, with a sharp knife and fingers, pull out the bones. This will leave you with butterflied fillets. Alternatively, you can ask your fishmonger to do this for you. Lay the fish on a board, skin-side up, and allow the skin to dry out a little while you prepare the rest of the dish.

To make the salmorejo, put the tomatoes in a blender with the bread, garlic, vinegar and olive oil. Season well and blitz, adding a little cold water to loosen. Season again to taste and chill in the fridge.

Cook the eggs in boiling water for 6–7 minutes, then cool under cold water.

To make the croutons, fry the bread in olive oil with the lemon thyme until golden and crisp. Sprinkle with sea salt and drain on kitchen paper.

Line a wok with foil and scatter with a few wood chips and the herbs. Press a wire rack over the top of the wood chips in the wok, ensuring it fits inside snugly. Place the fish skin-side down on the rack, then cover the top with a lid or more foil, to stop the smoke from escaping. Place over a medium heat and, as soon as plumes of smoke have started to appear, smoke for 10–15 minutes, until cooked through. Sprinkle with the fruit vinegar.

Peel and slice the eggs. Pour the soup into wide bowls and top with the croutons, egg slices, smoked sardine fillets and a good drizzle of extra-virgin olive oil.

Snails with chilli, tomato & garlic

Serves 6–8

Snails are common in Mediterranean cuisine, however *cabrillas* is a variety of snail that's abundant in drier regions, such as La Janda in Cádiz, and the land surrounding Seville. They are completely different in both looks and flavour to other snails; they have a beautifully striped shell and a more delicate taste. If you buy them live, you'll need to purge the snails a few days before cooking. I usually feed them carrots, but ask your supplier their preferred method and instructions, then follow to the letter. I serve this dish with bread and a glass of Oloroso sherry, as it has enough body to keep up with the chilli.

1 kg (2 lb 3 oz) live and purged snails
1 tablespoon extra-virgin olive oil
1 onion, finely chopped
2 carrots, finely chopped
2 garlic cloves, finely chopped
sea salt and freshly ground black pepper
4 large ripe tomatoes, peeled and finely chopped
1–2 red chillies, deseeded and finely chopped
½ teaspoon chilli flakes
1 litre (34 fl oz/4 cups) fish or vegetable stock

Wash the snails under cold water in a colander and discard any where the shell has broken. Soak in a bowl of cold water for 20 minutes, then drain.

Bring a large pan of water to the boil. Drop the snails into the boiling water. Bring back to the boil then remove from the heat drain well.

Pour the oil into a large saucepan over a medium heat and fry the onion, carrots and garlic with a good pinch of salt and pepper for 7 minutes, until softened. Add the tomatoes, chilli, chilli flakes and the snails, then pour over the stock. Bring to the boil and simmer for 45 minutes. Remove from the heat, taste for seasoning and serve with bread and a glass of white wine.

Grilled octopus with asparagus, broad beans & blackened lemon

Serves 4

On our research trip, we'd had a few days of rain, when it suddenly stopped. We were walking along the Granada coast in Salobreña when we came across a *chiringuito* (a kind of small bar) in La Playa El Peñón, where, for the first time in what felt like a long time, we had the most amazing views of the sunset, cloud-free. We also ate some incredible grilled octopus. Paco, who runs the *chiringuito* with his cousins, is the third generation – his grandfather opened it in 1954. I can definitely recommend it as a place to enjoy good food, company and views.

1 small leek, halved
2 celery stalks, roughly chopped
1 onion, halved
1 carrot, roughly chopped
3 garlic cloves, peeled
1 whole octopus, weighing
   1.5–1.7 kg (3 lb 5–12 oz)
extra-virgin olive oil,
   for griddling
sea salt and freshly ground
   black pepper

For the asparagus and beans
500 g (1 lb 2 oz) asparagus
3 tablespoons extra-virgin olive
   oil, plus extra for drizzling
sea salt and freshly ground
   black pepper
2 lemons, halved
225 g (8 oz) podded broad
   (fava) beans
1 tablespoon sherry vinegar
handful of fresh oregano, mint
   and parsley leaves, chopped

Place the vegetables and garlic in a large saucepan, cover with water and bring to a boil. Once boiling, use tongs to quickly plunge the octopus into the water three times; this helps to keep the tentacles from touching each other. Once plunged, lower the octopus into the water and cook gently for 30 minutes, until tender. Remove the octopus from the water, allow to cool, then cut the tentacles from the body.

Heat a griddle pan over a high heat. Rub the asparagus with olive oil and season well. When the griddle pan starts to smoke, add the lemon halves and asparagus and griddle for 2–3 minutes, turning occasionally, until they blacken. Add the broad beans with the 3 tablespoons of extra-virgin olive oil and sherry vinegar. Cook for 2 minutes then remove from the heat. Drain away the oil and vinegar, then mix the beans and asparagus with the chopped herbs in a shallow serving bowl or plate.

Brush the octopus tentacles in oil and sear on the griddle for 4–5 minutes. Remove from the pan and slice. Drizzle with extra-virgin olive oil and sea salt.

Add the octopus to the asparagus and broad beans. Squeeze over the juice from the blackened lemons, splash over more extra-virgin olive oil, season well and serve.

Mojama & pickled apple salad

Serves 4

1 green apple, cored and
    finely sliced
½ cucumber, cored and finely
    sliced into half moons
70 ml (2⅓ fl oz/⅓ cup) white
    wine vinegar
70 ml (2⅓ fl oz/⅓ cup) water
1 teaspoon fennel seeds
2 teaspoons caster (superfine)
    sugar
3 tablespoons extra-virgin olive
    oil, plus extra for drizzling
sea salt and freshly ground
    black pepper
handful of blanched almonds
150 g (5 oz) mojama, finely
    sliced
75 g (2½ oz) baby salad leaves

Mojama is simply another way to eat tuna; in the old days,
salting the fish was a common preserving method. Usually
the loin of the tuna, it's served thinly sliced and is very
popular in Cádiz and Huelva, where they eat it just with
toasted almonds.

Place the apple and cucumber into a medium bowl.

Pour the vinegar and water into a small saucepan and add
the fennel seeds and caster sugar. Gently melt the sugar
over a medium heat, then bring to a boil and pour over the
apple and cucumber. Leave to stand for 10–15 minutes, then
drain and toss with the extra-virgin olive oil and seasoning,
to taste.

Toast the almonds in a dry pan, then roughly slice.

Arrange the pickled apple and cucumber with the mojama
slices, baby salad leaves and toasted almonds on individual
plates and serve with an extra drizzle of oil.

Monkfish skewers with lentils

Serves 4

I have been cooking this dish for many years, but it was with great surprise that I found it on the menu at El Peñón in Salobreña. Paco, the chef, was doing a great job keeping an eye on all the different skewers he was cooking – maybe 25 at any given time, all grilled to perfection.

200 g (7 oz/1 cup) brown lentils
sea salt and freshly ground
  black pepper
5 vine-ripened tomatoes
1 onion, finely chopped
4 garlic cloves, finely sliced
2 teaspoons pimentón de la
  Vera
few sprigs of thyme, leaves
  picked
olive oil, for frying
600 g (1 lb 5 oz) monkfish, cut
  into cubes
12 large raw shell-on prawns
  (shrimp)
1 green (bell) pepper, cut into
  chunks
1 courgette (zucchini), cut into
  chunks
1 red onion, cut into thin wedges
extra-virgin olive oil, for drizzling

Place the lentils in a medium saucepan with a generous pinch of salt and cover with cold water. Bring to a boil and simmer gently for 20 minutes, until almost cooked.

Meanwhile, peel the tomatoes by scoring a cross in the base of each. Place in a bowl and cover in just-boiled water. Leave for 30 seconds, remove and plunge into cold water. Peel the skins, and roughly chop the flesh.

In a frying pan over a medium heat, gently cook the onion and garlic with the pimentón and thyme in a little olive oil for 10 minutes, until softened. Add the tomatoes and season well. Drain the lentils and add to the tomato pan with a splash of the cooking liquid and cook for 5 minutes, until the lentils are tender.

Meanwhile, light a charcoal barbecue and add some kindling to get it nice and hot and full of flames, then wait for it to cool to a medium heat. You can also use a griddle pan on the stove. Thread the fish, prawns and vegetables onto metal or wooden skewers (if using wooden skewers, soak them in warm water for 30 minutes beforehand). Drizzle with olive oil and season, then sear for 2–3 minutes on each side, until the fish is cooked and the vegetables are tender and a little charred.

Serve the lentils topped with the skewers and a good drizzle of extra-virgin olive oil.

Ajo colorao (my way) with baked bream

Serves 4

This is a recipe from the Almeńa and Córdoba region; normally it's more stew-like and the predominant spice is cumin, but I just love using saffron with fish, too. And what can I say about the crispy capers – this is definitely my spin on things, but the base recipe is true to the original, despite my little twists.

600 g (1 lb 5 oz) potatoes, peeled and chopped
2 dried choricero peppers, roughly torn
sea salt and freshly ground black pepper
2 large vine-ripened tomatoes
1 teaspoon cumin seeds
pinch of saffron, soaked for 5 minutes in 2 tablespoons boiling water
2 garlic cloves, crushed
150 ml (5 fl oz/⅔ cup) fish stock
2 sea bream (about 500 g/ 1 lb 2 oz each), scaled and gutted
pared zest and juice of 1 orange
2–3 orange leaves or 2 bay leaves
few sprigs of lemon thyme
extra-virgin olive oil, for drizzling
2 tablespoons capers

Place the potatoes in a saucepan with the choricero peppers, cover with cold salted water and bring to a boil. Simmer gently for 15 minutes, then add the tomatoes and simmer for a further 5–10 minutes, until the potatoes are tender. Drain well and skin the tomatoes.

Place the peppers, skinned tomatoes, cumin, saffron and garlic into a small food processor or pestle and mortar and blend to a paste. Mash the potatoes with this paste and a good splash of fish stock. Season well.

Meanwhile, heat the oven to 180°C (350°F/Gas 4).

Place the fish in a roasting tin and tuck the orange zest, orange or bay leaves and thyme into the cavities. Drizzle with the orange juice and some olive oil and roast for 15–20 minutes until just cooked; the fins should pull out easily when they are ready.

Place the capers in a frying pan over a medium-high heat with a little oil and fry until crispy. Drain on kitchen paper.

Debone the fish and serve the flesh with the mashed potatoes, the crispy capers and a drizzle of extra-virgin olive oil.

Remojón Granadino

Serves 4

Remojón Granadino is a rural dish typical of La Alpujarra, with a distinct Moorish heritage. A very simple salad of orange and salt cod, the combination of sweet and salt makes this a little bit special. I like to keep a good hit of saltiness in the fish in this recipe, so often I just break it into small pieces and soak it for 1 hour, changing the water a couple of times and drying well after.

I tried this at Las Tinajas restaurant in Granada after visiting the Alhambra; walking around the Moorish palace and fortress was very atmospheric, and the perfect precursor to this historic dish.

400 g (14 oz) salt cod
3 oranges
2 free-range eggs
100 g (3½ oz) black olives, pitted
3 spring onions (scallions), finely sliced
freshly ground black pepper
1 tablespoon chopped chives
extra-virgin olive oil, for drizzling

Soak the salt cod in cold water for 24–48 hours, changing the water regularly. Test after 24 hours and see how salty it is – if it is still very salty, then keep soaking. It should be mildly salty and sweet to taste, and easily tearable when it is ready. Drain and flake into small pieces.

Slice the skin from the oranges and segment them, discarding the membranes but keeping 2 tablespoons of the juice.

Boil the eggs for 6–7 minutes, then cool under cold running water. Peel and cut into quarters.

To serve, arrange the oranges and eggs on a platter, top with the salt cod and scatter over the olives and spring onions. Season the reserved orange juice with black pepper and whisk in the chives and lots of extra-virgin olive oil, then drizzle over the salad.

Tuna tartar

Serves 4

The tuna caught off the Cádiz coast is some of the best in the world, and the fishing technique used is called *almadraba*. An age-old Phoenician method, it creates a maze of nets that the tuna swim into, taking advantage of their migration from the Atlantic to the Mediterranean for mating season.

If you are in Andalusia, the best restaurant to eat tuna tartar in is called La Carboná in Jerez. It's also a good place to try a wine called Parajete, apparently a favourite of Shakespeare's.

½ small red onion, very finely chopped
400 g (14 oz) sushi grade albacore or yellow fin tuna, cut into 1 cm (½ in) dice
1 serrano or jalepeño chilli, deseeded and finely chopped
1 tablespoon capers, rinsed and chopped
1 avocado, peeled, stone removed and cut into 1 cm (½ in) dice
juice of 1–2 limes
sea salt and freshly ground black pepper
2 tablespoons extra-virgin olive oil
handful of coriander (cilantro) leaves, chopped

Place the red onion in a small bowl and cover with cold water. Soak for 5 minutes to remove some of the harsh flavour. Drain well.

In a medium bowl, mix the tuna with the onion, chilli, capers, avocado and lime juice to taste. Season well, drizzle over the extra-virgin olive oil and toss with the coriander. Serve immediately.

VEGETABLES

During the Al-Andalus period, there were several developments, improvements and introductions of new strategies to Spain's agriculture, which helped to grow crops in arid areas using systems that redistributed water and controlled exactly where it went.

Another event that had a huge impact on the produce grown in the country was Christopher Columbus' discovery of America: vegetables and fruit such as potatoes, peppers, tomatoes, pineapples, avocados and mangoes were brought back with him to Spain, and as a result, you can find many tropical plants on the Granada coast.

Nowadays, Andalusia exports a lot of its fruit and vegetables to the rest of the world and is considered the pantry of Europe.

Beetroot, blood orange, pomegranate & goat's cheese salad
with membrillo dressing

Serves 6–8

In the main square of Aracena there is a great cheese shop, Monte Robledo, and the owner Maria Jesús is always very helpful when it comes to choosing cheese for this salad. In addition to running the shop, they also have a farm and make most of the cheese they sell – so if anyone knows the product well, it's them! If you go here, do make sure to visit the mushroom shop next door, too.

6–8 baby beetroot (beets), unpeeled
sprig of rosemary, leaves picked
4 blood oranges or 2 large oranges
seeds from ½ large pomegranate
a mix of sharp, peppery and bitter salad leaves, such as frisée, sorrel, radicchio and rocket (arugula)
50 g (2 oz) goat's cheese, such as Payoyo

For the dressing
5 tablespoons extra-virgin olive oil
2 tablespoons sherry vinegar
115 g (4 oz) membrillo (quince paste), chopped
sea salt and freshly ground black pepper

Preheat the oven to 190°C (375°F/Gas 5).

Wrap the beetroot individually in foil with the rosemary leaves, then roast for 35–40 minutes, until tender. When cool enough to handle, peel and cut into wedges.

Meanwhile, segment the oranges. Using a serrated knife, cut the peel away without digging too much into the flesh of the orange. Once peeled, run the knife in and out around the orange segments, leaving the membrane behind. Do this over a bowl to catch any juice, then place the cut segments in another bowl. Squeeze the leftover membrane into the bowl with the juice then discard.

Crack the seeds and juice from the pomegranate into the bowl with the orange juice, discarding the membrane.

To make the dressing, whisk the olive oil in a small bowl with the sherry vinegar. Add the orange juice and pomegranate, then mix in the chopped membrillo. Add more vinegar to sharpen if it seems too sweet and season to taste.

Arrange the beetroot and blood oranges on a serving plate with the salad leaves. Generously spoon the dressing over and finally shave over the cheese.

Aubergines with chestnut honey

Serves 6–8 as tapas or a side

Traditionally, fried aubergine tapas are served with *melaza*, or molasses, but one evening I realised I'd run out, so used chestnut honey instead, and it worked very well. This is Arabic in origin; at one time, sugar and honey were luxury products, so this was a very indulgent dish indeed.

2 large aubergines (eggplants)
fine sea salt
olive oil, for frying
110 g (4 oz/scant 1 cup) plain
   (all-purpose) flour
2 egg whites
2 tablespoons dark chestnut
   honey
150–200 g (5–7 oz) soft sheep's
   cheese, to serve
2 heads fresh lavender flowers,
   stripped

Trim and cut the aubergines into chunky 5 cm (2 in) batons. Try to make them roughly the same size as they will fry more evenly. Toss the aubergines with 1 teaspoon fine sea salt and leave to drain in a colander for 30 minutes. Pat dry with kitchen paper.

Pour 4 cm (½ in) olive oil into a pan and set over a medium heat. Sift the flour into a bowl with a pinch of salt, make a well in the centre and add 150 ml (5 fl oz/⅔ cup) cold water, a little at a time, gradually mixing with the flour until you have a smooth batter. In a separate bowl, whisk the egg whites to soft peaks, then fold them into the batter. Dip the aubergine into the batter and fry for 2 minutes on each side until crisp and golden; you will need to do this in batches so as not to overcrowd the pan.

Remove the aubergines one by one onto kitchen towel, then arrange on a plate and drizzle with the honey. Serve alongside soft, creamy sheep's cheese and sprinkle with the lavender flowers.

Pipirrana

Serves 4–6

Somewhere between a gazpacho and a salad, *pipirrana* is so wonderfully fresh. Perfect for summer, it can be eaten on toast or as a salad served with fish. In some areas, such as Málaga, people add octopus. Supposedly, this comes from La Alpujarra Granadina, a little group of villages on the south side of the Sierra Nevada mountains. These villages, Capileira, Pampaneira and Bubión, still have the charm of the old days.

6 free-range eggs
500 g (1 lb 2 oz) ripe tomatoes
2–3 green chillies, deseeded
2 red (bell) peppers, deseeded
4 spring onions (scallions), trimmed
1 large cucumber, peeled and deseeded
handful of garlic or chive flowers (optional)

For the dressing
2 tablespoons sherry vinegar
½ teaspoon caster (superfine) sugar
50 ml (2 fl oz/¼ cup) extra-virgin olive oil
sea salt and freshly ground black pepper

To serve
crusty bread

Boil the eggs for 6–7 minutes, then cool under cold water and set aside. These can be cooked up to 4 hours ahead.

Peel the tomatoes by scoring a cross in the base of each. Place in a bowl and cover in just-boiled water. Leave for 30 seconds, remove and plunge into cold water. Peel the skins.

Chop all the salad ingredients separately and toss gently in a salad bowl.

Whisk together the dressing ingredients until emulsified and season to taste. Stir through the salad. The salad is robust enough to sit in its dressing until you are ready to serve; the flavours will only enhance.

Peel and chop the eggs and add to the bowl at the last minute, then scatter with the flowers, if using. Serve with crusty bread.

Huevos a la flamenca

Serves 4

In my opinion, this is a perfect breakfast, brunch, lunch or dinner, popular throughout Andalusia. I tried to find out the exact origin of this, but it was impossible as there are so many different varieties, and so many places laying claim to it. Sometimes I add some crispy ham on top, and it's definitely improved with good bread and a glass of red wine on the side.

olive oil, for frying
1 aubergine (eggplant), diced
150 g (5 oz) cooking chorizo, diced (optional)
1 large onion, finely chopped
2 garlic cloves, crushed
good pinch of chilli flakes
1 teaspoon cumin seeds
600 g (1 lb 5 oz) large vine ripe tomatoes, chopped
2 roasted red (bell) peppers or 4 piquillo peppers, sliced
sea salt and freshly ground black pepper
4 free-range eggs

To serve
crusty bread

Preheat the oven to 200°C (400°F/Gas 6).

Pour a good ½ cm (¼ in) olive oil in a frying pan over a medium heat and gently cook the aubergine for 10 minutes, until golden and tender. Remove from the pan with a slotted spoon and set aside.

Add the chorizo, if using, to the pan and fry until golden and all the fat has been released, about 5 minutes. Scoop out with the slotted spoon and set aside.

Add the onion to the pan, drizzling in a little extra oil if you didn't use the chorizo, and cook for 10 minutes until soft, then add the garlic, chilli flakes and cumin seeds and cook for a couple of minutes before adding the tomatoes and peppers. Return the aubergine and chorizo to the pan along with a splash of water and season well. Cook over a low heat until the sauce is lovely and thick, about 10–15 minutes.

Tip the mixture into an ovenproof terracotta dish, spreading evenly. Make 4 hollows in the sauce and crack an egg into each. Pop the dish into the oven and bake for 15 minutes, until the eggs are just set. Serve immediately with crusty bread.

Pisto & egg empanadas

Serves 8

People from the centre of Spain go to the beach at the weekend in summer, usually on Sunday, and take a picnic. Empanadas are a great option for this, as are traditional tortilla, because you can eat them cold.

1 aubergine (eggplant), diced
    into 1.5 cm (1 in) cubes
extra-virgin olive oil,
    for roasting and frying
2 medium free-range eggs
3 large tomatoes
2 onions, finely sliced
3 garlic cloves, crushed
2 teaspoons ground cumin
1 red (bell) pepper, sliced
sea salt and freshly ground
    black pepper
handful of flat-leaf parsley,
    finely chopped
finely grated zest of ½ lemon

For the pastry
350 g (12 oz/3 cups) plain
    (all-purpose) flour
½ teaspoon fine sea salt
170 g (6 oz) unsalted butter,
    cubed
1 free-range egg, plus 1 egg,
    beaten, to glaze
1–2 tablespoons whole
    (full-fat) milk

Preheat the oven to 180°C (350°F/Gas 4). Drizzle the aubergines with oil and roast for 45 minutes–1 hour, until really tender.

Boil the eggs for 6–7 minutes, then cool under cold water and set aside.

Peel the tomatoes by scoring a cross in the base of each. Place in a bowl and cover in just-boiled water. Leave for 30 seconds, remove and plunge into cold water. Peel the skins, and roughly chop the flesh. Set aside.

Meanwhile, add a good amount of oil to a frying pan over a medium heat and gently cook the onions for 15 minutes, until really lovely and tender. Add the garlic and cumin and fry for 1 minute.

Stir in the pepper and tomatoes with plenty of seasoning and simmer for 15 minutes. Once the aubergines are tender, add to the pan and cook for a further 10 minutes. Season and mix in the parsley and lemon zest and set aside to cool.

Peel and roughly chop the eggs then stir into the cold veg mixture.

While the filling cooks, make the pastry. Whizz the flour and salt with the butter in a food processor, or rub into the flour with your fingers in a mixing bowl, until it resembles breadcrumbs. Add the egg and pulse or stir with a wooden spoon to bring it together, adding the milk if needed. Once it starts to clump, tip onto a clean work surface and knead into a smooth dough, 1–2 minutes. Flatten into a disc, wrap in cling film (plastic wrap) and chill for 15–20 minutes.

Turn the oven up to 200°C (400°F/Gas 6) and line a baking tray (pan) with baking paper.

Roll out the dough to 3–4 mm thick and cut out eight 12 cm (4¾ in) discs, rerolling the trimmings each time.

Divide the cold vegetable and egg mixture between the discs. Dampen the edges with water then fold one half over to meet the other to form a half moon. Crimp with your fingers and put onto a lined baking sheet. Brush all over with beaten egg, then bake for 15–20 minutes, until golden and crisp. Serve warm or at room temperature.

Ajillo with roasted leeks & grapes

Serves 6

Ajoblanco is a very popular gazpacho throughout Andalusia – a cold soup, perfect for a hot summer's day, that is usually garnished with grapes. I call this version *ajillo* because, although it's made with the same ingredients as an ajoblanco, it's a thicker, saucier version, which I have used here as a dressing for the grapes and baby leeks. It also makes a great garnish for grilled fish or can even be enjoyed just as a dip with bread.

12 baby leeks
200 g (7 oz) muscat grapes, halved
1 tablespoon extra-virgin olive oil, plus extra to serve
sea salt and freshly ground black pepper
5 tablespoons flaked almonds
sprig of fresh oregano, leaves picked

For the ajillo (makes 600 ml/ 20 fl oz/2½ cups)
90 g (3¼ oz) stale white bread
140 g (5 oz) blanched almonds, soaked overnight in 300 ml (10 fl oz/1¼ cups) water
2 tablespoons sherry vinegar
2 large garlic cloves
75 ml (2½ fl oz/⅓ cup) extra-virgin olive oil
good pinch of flaked sea salt

Preheat the oven to 200°C (400°F/Gas 6).

In a roasting tin, drizzle the leeks and grapes with olive oil and season well. Roast for 20–25 minutes, until the leeks are tender.

Meanwhile, soak the bread with the pre-soaked almonds in their water for 25 minutes. Using a small food processor or a pestle and mortar, blend the bread with the almonds, vinegar and garlic until you have a thick paste. Slowly mix in the olive oil until the sauce is completely smooth, adding water if it still needs loosening. Season with salt to taste.

Put the leeks and grapes on a platter and top with the toasted almonds. Drizzle over a little more oil, and sprinkle over the fresh oregano to serve.

Asparagus tortilla

Serves 4–6 as tapas

I always get so excited about the start of British asparagus season; I think I inherited this from my late dad, who loved going to pick asparagus, especially the wild variety. Walking around Aracena Sierra collecting wild asparagus, which grow randomly on the mountains, is an unforgettable thing.

150 ml (5 fl oz/⅔ cup) extra-virgin olive oil
1 onion, finely sliced
3 garlic cloves, finely chopped
2 bunches wild asparagus, or 250 g (9 oz) farmed asparagus, finely chopped
4 free-range eggs
sea salt and freshly ground black pepper

Pour a glug of the olive oil into a frying pan over a medium-low heat and cook the onion for 10–15 minutes until lovely and soft. Add the garlic and asparagus and cook over a high heat for 5 minutes until tender and golden. Remove from the heat and set aside.

In a medium bowl, beat the eggs, then add the asparagus mix and plenty of seasoning.

Pour the rest of the oil for the tortilla into an 18 cm (7 in) non-stick frying pan over a high heat. When the oil is hot, add the egg mixture. Swirl the pan until the mixture starts to set around the edges, then reduce the heat and cook for 4–5 minutes, until the tortilla just starts to set, so the bottom and sides are golden but the middle is still quite loose.

Cover the pan with a flat lid or board and turn the tortilla carefully onto it. Don't worry that it is still quite runny, it will all come back together when you continue to cook it. Slide the tortilla back into the pan and, over a low heat, use a spatula to tuck the edges under to give it its characteristic curved look. Cook for 2 minutes, then turn onto a board and serve. It should still be lovely and juicy in the middle when you cut into it.

Warm carrot & fennel salad

Serves 4

I ordered something similar to this as a side dish in La Duquesa, Medina Sidonia, and thought the combination of just-tender carrots and aromatics was amazing. Part of the Moorish legacy is the use of spices such as cinnamon, cumin and cardamom in Spain; they are not cooked with often, but it's something that I love to explore and learn about. If the carrots have leaves, keep them to one side, because you can use them as a garnish to finish the dish. At my restaurant Pizarro, we fry the carrots in fat from jamón Ibérico.

12–15 baby carrots, halved lengthways if large, scrubbed and leafy tops reserved
3 tablespoons extra-virgin olive oil
1 tablespoon fennel seeds
2 teaspoons sherry vinegar
sea salt and freshly ground black pepper

Place the carrots in a saucepan of boiling water for 1–2 minutes, then drain.

In a large frying pan over a medium heat, warm the oil with the fennel seeds for 2 minutes, until fragrant. Add the carrots to the pan and toss to coat in the oil. Sprinkle over the vinegar and toss again. Cook for 2–3 minutes so that the flavours merge and the carrots soften.

Season with salt and pepper and stir through the leafy tops. Spoon into a serving dish, making sure the fennel and oil comes with the carrots, and eat warm.

Potatoes, peppers, onion & vinegar

Serves 6 as a side or tapas

One of the most popular tapas in Seville is *papas aliñás*, and the very best version is served at Bodeguita Romero, a traditional tavern in the city centre. It was opened many years ago by Mr Antonio Romero, and nowadays is run by his son Pedro Romero and his wife Ángeles, but Antonio still makes this dish in the kitchen every day.

2 kg (4 lbs 6½ oz) new season
   potatoes, such as Charlotte,
   scrubbed
sea salt
2 green (bell) peppers,
   deseeded and finely sliced
1 bunch spring onions
   (scallions), finely chopped
100 ml (3½ fl oz/scant ½ cup)
   sherry vinegar
200 ml (7 fl oz/¾ cup) extra-
   virgin olive oil

Place the potatoes in a pan of cold salted water and bring to a boil. Cook for 25–30 minutes, until tender, then drain.

While still hot, remove the skins of the potatoes and break them up into pieces. Tip into a bowl and add the peppers, spring onions, vinegar, extra-virgin olive oil and plenty of salt. Toss well. Taste, add more vinegar, oil or salt if you think it needs it, and serve.

Orange & oregano salad

Serves 4

This salad is one of the simplest recipes in the book; it's full of flavour, but relies on very good ingredients. The weather in Andalusia means oranges from there are truly fantastic – you will also need a really peppery olive oil. This is lovely as a side to grilled fish or meat, and perfect to serve with *Espeto* on page 84.

3 large sweet Navel oranges
4 tablespoons extra-virgin
    olive oil
1 teaspoon dried oregano
sea salt and freshly ground
    black pepper

Using a serrated knife, cut the skin and pith from the oranges. Slice into 1 cm (½ in) discs and place on a platter. Drizzle with the olive oil and sprinkle over the oregano and salt and pepper, then serve.

Cheese-stuffed fried olives

Serves 4 as a tapas

Olives trees are inextricably linked to Mediterranean culture, with olive oil being one of the main ingredients in our cuisine. In fact, although there are 300 million olive trees in Spain, only 5 per cent of those are eaten, the rest are used for making olive oil. When you think of all the olives eaten, it makes sense – yes, they are very common, but they should be given more credit as a high quality product. Gordales are one of my favourite varieties; *gorda* means fat and, indeed, these olives are plump and almost meaty.

12–16 gordal olives, pitted
70 g (2½ oz) semi-cured manchego, grated
2 tablespoons plain (all-purpose) flour
2 free-range eggs, lightly beaten
100 g (3½ oz/¾ cup) panko or dried breadcrumbs
olive oil, for frying
sea salt

To serve
cold sherry, preferably fino or manzanilla

Stuff the olives with as much manchego as you can fit inside them. Place the flour, egg and breadcrumbs in three separate shallow bowls. Roll the olives in the flour, then in the beaten egg, and finally in the breadcrumbs.

Heat 2 cm (1 in) oil in a deep saucepan to 180°C (350°F) – or until a cube of bread browns in about 20 seconds. Lower the olives into the oil and fry for a few minutes until golden brown. Drain on kitchen paper, season with sea salt and serve with a cold glass of sherry.

Calamares del campo

Serves 4

Calamares del campo, or field squid, is a funny name for onion and pepper rings that Andalusian people use – and by their shape and appearance, you can see why.

2 free-range egg whites
150 ml (5 fl oz/⅔ cup) chilled sparkling water
75 g (2½ oz/¾ cup) plain (all-purpose) flour
good pinch of hot smoked pimentón de la Vera, plus extra to serve
fine sea salt
olive oil or vegetable oil, for frying
2 onions, sliced into rounds and rings separated
1 red (bell) pepper, sliced into rounds about ½ cm (¼ in) thick
1 green (bell) pepper, sliced into rounds about ½ cm (¼ in) thick

In a bowl, whisk the egg whites until they form soft peaks. Sift the flour into a bowl with the pimentón and salt then add the sparkling water to form a smooth batter. Fold in the egg whites until fully incorporated.

Heat 2 cm (1 in) oil in a deep saucepan to 180°C (350°F) – or until a cube of bread browns in about 20 seconds. Dip the vegetable rings into the batter and lower straight into the hot oil. Fry for 2–3 minutes, until golden and cooked through. Drain on kitchen paper and serve hot with a scattering of salt and an extra pinch of pimentón.

Chickpea & spinach stew

Serves 4

Before and during Easter, Catholic people don't eat meat on Fridays, so this vegetarian stew, traditionally eaten during this period, has a long history, with distinct nods to the Moorish culture that predated Catholicism. According to some historians, this religious prohibition was merely a way for the church to control the consumption of an essential product by the masses, as meat was still on the table for the rich. Regardless, this stew is warming, filling, and wonderful to eat at any time of the year.

olive oil, for frying
100 g (3½ oz) stale bread, cut into chunks
60 g (2 oz) blanched almonds
2 teaspoons cumin seeds
good pinch of cayenne pepper
5 black peppercorns
1 onion, finely sliced
3 garlic cloves, crushed
600 g (1 lb 5 oz) ripe tomatoes, chopped
sea salt and freshly ground black pepper
700 g (1 lb 8½ oz) jar chickpeas (garbanzo beans)
2 large handfuls of baby spinach
4 slices of bread
100 g (3½ oz) manchego, grated

To serve
extra-virgin olive oil

Pour a little oil into a frying pan over a medium heat and fry the stale bread chunks for 3–4 minutes, until lightly browned. Add the almonds and spices and toast for 1 minute, then tip into a food processor and whizz with a splash of water to form a paste.

Heat a little more oil in the pan and gently cook the onion for 10 minutes, until softened. Add the garlic and tomatoes and season well. Bubble for 20 minutes, then add the chickpeas along with their liquid from the jar. Add the bread and almond paste and bring to the boil, then simmer for a few minutes to thicken before adding the spinach and letting it wilt. Check the seasoning and keep warm.

Heat the grill to medium-high. Drizzle the bread with oil and toast on one side, then flip over and lightly toast the other side. Top with the cheese and return to the grill to melt.

Spoon the stew into individual bowls and serve with the cheese toasts and a drizzle of extra-virgin olive oil.

Andrajos

Serves 4

This is a very strange name for a dish, because *andrajos* translates as 'dirty and bad dress'… but that's a long way from how it tastes, of course. This is great served either hot or cold, and works well with meat and fish, although you'll find it most commonly served with cod.

200 g (7 oz/1⅓ cups) plain (all-purpose) flour, plus extra for dusting
sea salt and freshly ground black pepper
100–120 ml (3½–4 fl oz/⅓–½ cup) water
olive oil, for frying
1 large onion, finely chopped
3 garlic cloves, finely sliced
1 red (bell) pepper, deseeded and roughly chopped
2 potatoes, peeled and diced
4 ripe tomatoes, finely chopped
good pinch of saffron, soaked in 2 tablespoons boiling water for 5 minutes
1 teaspoon ground cumin
½ teaspoon smoked pimentón de la Vera
1 litre (34 fl oz/4 cups) vegetable stock

To serve
crusty bread

In a large bowl, mix the flour with a pinch of salt and enough of the water to make a stiff but pliable dough. Divide into 4 pieces and leave to rest while you make the soup.

Pour a little olive oil into a wide, deep frying pan or large casserole dish over a medium heat and gently cook the onion for 10 minutes, until softened. Add the garlic, pepper and potatoes. Pour in the tomatoes and spices and cook for 1 minute. Add the stock and plenty of seasoning. Bring to the boil then simmer for 10–12 minutes, until the potatoes are nearly cooked.

On a lightly floured work surface, roll out the rested dough balls as thinly as possible into large circles, then add these to the pan. Cook for 8–10 minutes, until cooked, then use forks to shred them into rags. Serve the soup with crusty bread.

Artichokes, jamón Ibérico & egg yolk

Serves 4–6

The first time I visited my friends at Cinco Jotas, they took me to a bar called José Vicente in Aracena, run by a man of the same name, where I first tried this dish. Since then I've been back many times, and we've become firm friends. The last time I saw him, he opened the restaurant just for me and a group of ten friends, single-handedly running the kitchen and serving our table for the evening.

½ lemon
small bunch of flat-leaf parsley
5–6 baby artichokes
1 tablespoon extra-virgin
   olive oil
50 g (2 oz) jamón Ibérico, cut
   into thin strips
1 garlic clove
sea salt and freshly ground
   black pepper
2 free-range egg yolks

First, fill a small bowl with water and squeeze in the juice from the lemon half. Leave the lemon half in the water and add a few sprigs of the parsley.

Peel off the first 3 layers of outer leaves from the artichokes then trim the stalk to about 3 cm (1¼ in) long. With a small, sharp knife, trim the top half of the artichoke, then peel around the sides with a vegetable peeler until you are left with the paler, central part of the choke. Cut into quarters then place in the bowl of lemon water.

Pour the olive oil into a frying pan over a medium heat and add the artichokes. Fry them for 10 minutes until golden and tender. Add half of the jamón and fry for 2–3 minutes, until just crisp, then stir through the garlic for 1 minute. Add half the parsley to the pan, season everything really well, then tip into a bowl. Toss through the egg yolks until sticky and add the remaining jamón and parsley to serve.

Swiss chard rice with mushroom toasts

Serves 6

Apparently rice was introduced to Andalusia in the Visigoths period, around 1,700 years ago. Today, Andalusia is the one of the biggest producers of rice in Spain, and in 2017, the areas where it was grown around Seville and Cádiz and represented almost 50 per cent of the national production.

olive oil, for frying
1 large onion, finely sliced
4 garlic cloves, finely sliced
2 dried choricero peppers, torn and soaked in boiling water for 15 minutes
2 bay leaves
generous pinch of saffron, soaked in 2 tablespoons of boiling water for 5 minutes
250 g (9 oz) Charlotte potatoes, peeled and diced
300 g (10½ oz/1½ cups) bomba rice or other short-grain rice
1.3 litres (44 fl oz/5½ cups) vegetable stock
250 g (9 oz) Swiss chard, sliced
sea salt and freshly ground black pepper

For the toasts
3 tablespoons olive oil
200 g (7 oz) wild mushrooms, cleaned and chopped
2–3 tablespoons creamy goat's cheese
50 g (2 oz) manchego, grated
sea salt and freshly ground black pepper
6 pieces of toast

Pour a little oil into a casserole dish over a medium heat and gently cook the onion for 10 minutes, until softened. Add the garlic and choricero peppers and cook for 1 minute more.

Add the bay leaves, saffron, potatoes and rice, toss to coat in the oil and then pour over 1 litre (34 fl oz/4 cups) of the stock. Season well and cook, covered, for 20–25 minutes, adding the rest of the stock 10 minutes before the end of cooking along with the Swiss chard. Season to taste.

To make the toasts, pour the olive oil into a frying pan over a high heat and cook the mushrooms for a few minutes, until browned and any juices have evaporated. Tip into a food processor with the goat's cheese and manchego, season well and pulse to form a coarse pâté.

Spread the toasts with the mushroom pâté and serve with the Swiss chard rice.

Strawberry gazpacho

Serves 6

It is undeniable that gazpacho is one of the star dishes of Andalusia. When I travelled to Málaga, I discovered that they add fruits such as grapes and melon to make it more nutritious and complex in flavour. Strawberry gazpacho sounds like an unusual incarnation of the traditional recipe, but the berries are very popular in Huelva, and the result is just terrific.

300 g (10½ oz) vine-ripened tomatoes, chopped
700 g (1 lb 8½ oz) ripe strawberries, with a few reserved for garnish
1 roasted red (bell) pepper, sliced
1 small shallot, finely chopped
1 small garlic clove, crushed
1 tablespoon sherry vinegar
75 ml (2½ fl oz/⅓ cup) extra-virgin olive oil, plus extra for drizzling
sea salt and freshly ground black pepper
olive oil, for frying
2 slices sourdough, diced
basil leaves and edible flowers, to garnish

To serve
cold sherry, preferably amontillado or palo cortado

In a large bowl, combine all the ingredients except the olive oil, sourdough and garnishes and leave to infuse overnight.

The next day, add the olive oil and whizz together with a hand blender or in a food processor until smooth, adding a splash of water if it's too thick. Season to taste.

Pour a little olive oil into a frying pan over a medium heat and fry the sourdough croutons for 4–5 minutes, until golden. Drain on kitchen paper and sprinkle with sea salt.

Divide the gazpacho between individual soup bowls and garnish with basil leaves, edible flowers and croutons. Finish with a drizzle of extra-virgin olive oil and some sea salt. Serve with a cold glass of sherry.

DESSERTS

The Arabic influence in Andalusia is perhaps most prominent in traditional desserts – it was during the Moorish reign that sugar was introduced to Spain, as well as spices such as cinnamon, cardamom and saffron. Sugar and honey were luxury products, and their reputation influenced the cuisine in the rest of the peninsula. Bitter orange trees – known as Seville oranges – were originally used to decorate the streets and the patios, but now the marmalade made from this fruit has become indispensable in desserts, as well as on the breakfast table. Also of note are the age-old desserts and pastries made by the nuns of the region, and I was lucky enough to spend time in a convent learning the recipes from them.

Walnut, sherry & honey semifreddo

Serves 6–8

Semifreddo could not be easier to make. Here, it provides a great example of how just a few Andalusian ingredients can work very well together. If you'd prefer to go booze-free, you can just leave out the sherry.

olive oil, for greasing
4 medium free-range eggs, separated
1½ tablespoons Pedro Ximénez sherry
100 g (3½ oz/½ cup) caster (superfine) sugar
325 ml (11 fl oz/generous 1¼ cups) double (heavy) cream
85 g (3 oz) walnut halves, plus a handful to serve
1 tablespoon dark honey, plus extra for drizzling

Grease a 450 g (1 lb) loaf tin with olive oil and line with enough cling film (plastic wrap) that it hangs over the sides.

Place the egg yolks, sherry and sugar into a small bowl. Tip the egg whites into a separate large, clean and dry bowl and pour the cream into another large bowl.

In a small frying pan over a medium heat, toast the walnuts until lightly browned, then remove from the heat and crush lightly with the end of a rolling pin while still in the pan. Stir through the honey; it will fizz a little, but make sure it coats the walnuts well.

Beat the egg whites to stiff peaks with an electric whisk. With the same whisk, beat the egg yolk mixture until thick and forming a ribbon trail. Then, again with the same whisk, whip the cream to soft peaks.

With a large metal spoon, fold the cream into the egg yolk mixture, then gently fold in the egg whites until combined. Stir through the honeyed walnuts and spoon into the lined loaf tin, right to the top of the tin. Loosely lay a sheet of cling film over the top and then cover with a sheet of foil. Place in the freezer for a minimum of 5 hours before serving; it will keep in the freezer for up to 3 months.

To serve, toast a handful of walnut halves in a small frying pan over a medium heat and allow to cool a little. Turn out the semifreddo, peeling back the cling film and lift onto a board or platter. Top with toasted walnut halves and a good drizzle of dark honey.

Dark Seville orange marmalade with Pedro Ximénez

Makes 7 × 340 g (12 oz) jars

Orange trees were purely decorative in gardens and patios throughout Andalusia in years gone by, and very common in Arabic culture; they are still used in this way in Spanish cities, but especially Seville. I love to walk around Barrio de Santa Cruz when the oranges trees are in blossom. You almost feel intoxicated by the aroma. The fruit is really bitter and not for eating, but you can make the most amazing marmalade.

This recipe is from my dear friend Sarah Randell – her book *Marmalade: A Bittersweet Cookbook* is a must-buy.

1 kg (2 lb 3 oz) bitter Seville
   oranges
juice of 4 lemons
2 kg (4 lb 7 oz) demerara sugar
50 ml (2 fl oz/¼ cup) Pedro
   Ximénez sherry

Put the whole oranges into a saucepan and cover them with water. Bring to simmering point, then cook, covered, for 1½–2 hours, or until they give no resistance when pierced with the tip of a small sharp knife. Place the hot oranges into a bowl and tip the cooking liquid into a large measuring jug.

When the oranges have cooled a little, pierce them at one end so you can gently squeeze any excess juice into the measuring jug. There won't be a lot, but it saves the liquid escaping onto your chopping board.

Slice the oranges into 4–5 mm slices, discarding the buttons from the ends of the fruit and the pips. Put the slices into a preserving pan. Top up the liquid in the jug to 1.5 litres (50¾ fl oz/6⅓ cups) with water, then pour this into the preserving pan. Add the lemon juice and sugar.

Heat the marmalade over a low heat, stirring to dissolve the sugar. Bring everything up to a rolling boil and cook the marmalade for 30–40 minutes, or until setting point is reached. To test this, dip a wooden spoon into the marmalade, then hold it above the pan, turning it a few times. If the marmalade is set, it will drop from the spoon as a flake or sheet of drips. Alternatively, spoon a little marmalade onto a saucer, leave it to cool and if it wrinkles when pushed with a finger, it is ready.

Take the pan off the heat and stir in the sherry. Leave the marmalade to settle for 15 minutes before transferring it to hot sterilised jars. Seal and leave to cool completely before labelling.

Apricot sorbet with tejas dulces de Sevilla

Serves 8

The secret of any good sorbet is really ripe fruit, which means plenty of sunshine – and Andalusia certainly has that. Sugar was a luxury product in the Moorish period; some sugar plantations can still be found in areas with *cañaverales*, or reedbeds, in Málaga, but of course they are not as common as they used to be.

300 g (10½ oz/1½ cups) caster (superfine) sugar
350 ml (12 fl oz/1½ cups) water
1 kg (2 lb 3 oz) ripe apricots, stoned and halved
1 vanilla pod, scraped of its seeds
squeeze of lemon juice

For the tejas dulces de Sevilla
80 g (2¾ oz/⅓ cup) caster (superfine) sugar
2 egg whites
35 g (1¼ oz/¼ cup) plain (all-purpose) flour
1 tablespoon almond flour
50 g (2 oz) unsalted butter, melted and cooled
40 g (1½ oz) flaked almonds
icing (confectioner's) sugar, for dusting

To make the sorbet, mix the sugar and water in a very wide, deep frying pan and set over a low heat to melt. Once the sugar has dissolved, bring the mixture to the boil for 5 minutes. Add the apricots to the pan, cut-side down, along with the vanilla pod and its seeds. Simmer for 15 minutes, until the apricots have softened and the syrup is thick and glossy.

Allow to cool, then peel the skins from the apricots – they should slip off easily. Transfer the apricots and their syrup to a food processor and whizz until smooth. Add a squeeze of lemon and stir, pour into an airtight container, then cover and cool completely.

Fill the bowl of an ice cream machine with the apricot mixture and churn until you have a smooth sorbet. Spoon the mixture into a large airtight container and freeze, covered, for up to 3 months.

Preheat the oven to 170°C (340°F/Gas 4). Line a baking tray (pan) with baking paper.

To make the tejas, beat the caster sugar and egg whites with a fork in a medium mixing bowl until frothy. Sift over the flours and gently fold in with a metal spoon, then add the cooled melted butter.

Spoon teaspoon-sized dollops of the mixture onto the lined baking tray, sprinkle with flaked almonds and bake for 6–8 minutes, until lightly golden. Cool on the tray for 5 minutes, then transfer to a wire rack to cool completely. Dust with icing sugar.

Take the sorbet out of the freezer 10 minutes before serving. Scoop into bowls and serve with tejas dulces de Sevilla.

Jeannie's marmalade soufflé puddings with candied oranges

Serves 6

I was very inspired by the three days I spent in Finca Buenvino, a bed and breakfast just outside of Seville, in the remote area of the Sierra de Aracena and Picos de Aroche Natural Park in the Huelva region. The fertile land here provides all you need, and the produce in the local markets is unimaginably fresh. My hosts were Jeannie and her husband Sam, and their children Jago and Charlie. I'm very thankful to Jeannie for giving me this recipe. It is best made with the Dark Seville orange marmalade with Pedro Ximénez on page 186.

3 sheets of leaf gelatine
5 medium free-range eggs, separated
3–5 heaped tablespoons Seville orange marmalade
250 ml (8½ fl oz/1 cup) double (heavy) cream

For the candied oranges
peel from 3 large Navel oranges, finely sliced
100 g (3½ oz/½ cup) caster (superfine) sugar
100 ml (3½ fl oz/scant ½ cup) water
50 g (2 oz/¼ cup) granulated sugar

To make the candied oranges, cover the peel with cold water in a saucepan and bring to the boil. Drain and repeat this process with fresh water 3 times.

In a small saucepan over a medium heat, warm the caster sugar with the water until the sugar dissolves. Stir in the blanched orange peel and bring to a hard boil for 3 minutes, then take off the heat.

Drain the syrup off and shake any excess liquid from the peel. Spoon onto baking paper and sprinkle with the granulated sugar. Leave to set in a warm, dry place for 24 hours. You can store in a jam jar or another airtight container for up to 3 months.

To make the soufflés, first soak the gelatine in a bowl with 3 tablespoons of water until it softens, about 5 minutes.

Blitz the egg yolks in a food processor with the marmalade until almost smooth; if it's a mild marmalade you'll want to add more like 5 tablespoons, but 3 tablespoons of a strong and bitter marmalade will suffice.

In a medium mixing bowl, beat the egg yolk and marmalade mixture with an electric whisk to a ribbon consistency.

In a separate clean, dry bowl, whip the egg whites to soft stiff peaks with the electric whisk.

In another bowl, whip the cream with the electric whisk to soft peaks. Gently fold the yolks and cream together with a metal spoon, then fold into the egg whites, being careful not to knock out the air.

Heat the softened gelatine in its soaking water in a glass bowl over a small saucepan of simmering water, then once dissolved, gently fold it into the mixture. Stir so the gelatine is evenly distributed.

Divide the mixture, between six 150 ml (5 fl oz) glasses or ramekins and chill in the fridge for at least 1 hour, or up to 8 hours.

When ready to serve, sprinkle over the candied peel.

Gañotes

Serves 12

The last city I visited during my research for this book was Ronda, in Málaga. Ronda is stunning and, to my mind, one of the most beautiful towns in Andalusia, with a wealth of history and culture. I had the pleasure of meeting *las hermanas Franciscanas* – otherwise known as the Franciscan nuns. They were really generous in allowing me into the convent and teaching me their secret recipes. This is one of them.

150 g (5 oz/⅔ cup) caster (superfine) sugar
3 large free-range eggs
80 ml (2¾ fl oz/⅓ cup) extra-virgin olive oil
2 oranges: finely grated zest of 1; pared zest of 1, thinly sliced
finely grated zest of 1 lemon
500 g (1 lb 2 oz/4 cups) plain (all-purpose) flour
2 teaspoons ground cinnamon
1 tablespoon sesame seeds
1 tablespoon anise liqueur, such as Pernod
light olive oil, for deep-frying
100 ml (3½ fl oz/scant ½ cup) honey
1½ tablespoons water

In a large bowl, beat the sugar, eggs, olive oil and grated zests with a wooden spoon until smooth. Add the flour and mix to make a soft dough. Add the cinnamon, sesame seeds and liqueur and knead well for 2–5 minutes, until smooth and pliable.

Divide into 12 pieces. Roll each piece between your hands to form thin snakes of dough (about 1 cm/½ in thick), wrap around wooden gañotes moulds, or use the handles of wooden spoons, bearing in mind that the handles will be submerged in hot oil.

Heat 2 cm (1 in) oil in a deep saucepan to 180°C (350°F) – or until a cube of bread browns in about 20 seconds. Place the dough (with the wooden moulds) into the hot oil and cook for 5–6 minutes, until golden. Slide the gañotes off the moulds or spoon handles and drain on kitchen paper.

As they cook, warm the honey with the water in a small saucepan until syrupy. Serve with the hot gañotes.

Tortas de aceite

Serves 6

These crisp biscuits, made largely with extra-virgin olive oil, are a legacy of Spain's Moorish heritage. Arabs ruled the south of the country for a long time, during the period of Al-Andalus, until 1492, when Catholics conquered the Kingdom of Granada, the last Moorish state. During this period, the settlers came up with many inventions that have had a lasting impact on Spanish culture, but perhaps the most important was the Almazara (oil press) system – or, as I like to say, the extraction of liquid gold from olives.

olive oil, for greasing
1 tablespoon caster (superfine) sugar, plus extra for dusting
2 teaspoons demerara sugar
1 tablespoon fennel seeds
1 teaspoon fast-action dried yeast
80 ml (2¾ fl oz/⅓ cup) warm water
60 ml (2 fl oz/¼ cup) extra-virgin olive oil
160 g (5½ oz/1⅓ cups) plain (all-purpose) flour, plus extra for dusting
1 teaspoon sea salt
1 free-range egg white mixed with a little sea salt

Grease two large baking trays (pans) with olive oil and dust with caster sugar and 1 teaspoon of the demerara.

Preheat the oven to 220°C (430°F/Gas 7).

Toast the fennel seeds in a dry frying pan for 2 minutes, or until fragrant. Remove from the heat.

Mix the yeast with the warm water and half of the caster sugar. Set aside to froth a little. Stir through the extra-virgin olive oil.

In a large mixing bowl, whisk together the flour, fennel seeds and salt. Make a well in the centre and pour in the yeast mixture. Slowly incorporate it into the flour with a wooden spoon until you have a smooth dough that feels a little greasy.

Dust the work surface with flour and separate the dough into six 50 g (2 oz) balls. Roll each out to a disc about 12 cm (4¾ in) in diameter and lift onto the prepared trays, leaving a little space between each disc. Brush the tops with egg white, then sprinkle with a little more caster sugar and the remaining demerara. Bake in the oven for 10 minutes, or until golden and crisp. Swap the trays around halfway through cooking if the top one is browning quicker than the one below it.

Use a metal spatula to lift the discs off the trays and place them on a wire rack to cool and crisp up a little. Serve warm or at room temperature.

Santa Fé pionono with elderflower

Serves 12

Ceferino Isla is the creator of the *pionono*, and I'm sure he would be surprised to see how popular this gorgeous sweet has become in Granada. It first appeared in his café, Pastelería Casa Isla, in Santa Fé – a village close to the city – in honour of Pope Pio IX. You can find them easily in Granada at Pastelería Casa Isla. All along the Darro river in Granada, you can find plenty of elderflowers, which is why I've added the flavour to this version.

For the sponge
butter, for greasing
2 large eggs, separated
40 g (1⅓ oz/¼ cup) caster (superfine) sugar, plus extra for dusting
2 tablespoons plain (all-purpose) flour
2 tablespoons cornflour (cornstarch)
1½ teaspoons whole (full-fat) milk

For the cream
100 ml (3½ fl oz/scant ½ cup) whole (full-fat) milk
2 tablespoons double (heavy) cream
60 g (2¼ oz/⅓ cup) caster (superfine) sugar, plus extra to sprinkle
1 large egg
2 teaspoons plain (all-purpose) flour
finely grated zest of ½ lemon

First, make the cream. Pour the milk and cream into a saucepan over a medium heat and warm until steaming.

In a mixing bowl, whisk together the sugar and egg until thick and foamy, then fold in the flour and lemon zest. Pour over the hot milk mixture and whisk to combine. Return the mixture to the pan and cook over a low heat, whisking, for 3–5 minutes, until you have a thick patisserie cream. Spoon into a bowl and cover with cling film (plastic wrap) that touches the surface of the cream to stop a skin from forming, and allow to cool.

Preheat the oven to 200°C (400°F/Gas 6). Grease and line a 23 × 33 cm (8¾ × 13 in) Swiss roll tin with baking paper.

To make the sponge, in a mixing bowl, beat together the egg yolks and half the sugar with an electric whisk until thick and fluffy. Sift over the flours and fold in carefully with a metal spoon. Beat the egg whites with the remaining sugar to form stiff peaks, then fold these into the mixture with the milk. Spoon into the prepared tin and smooth out, then bake for 8–10 minutes until lightly golden and an inserted skewer comes out clean. Cool for a couple of minutes, then dust a clean tea towel with sugar and turn the sponge out onto it. Very carefully remove the baking paper. Using the tea towel, roll up the sponge (along the long side) and leave to cool completely.

To make the syrup, heat the water with the sugar and cordial in a pan until the sugar has dissolved. Bubble for a few minutes until syrupy, then add the St-Germain liqueur, if using.

Unroll the sponge and spread with a thin layer of the cream. Re-roll and cut into 2.5 cm (1 in) portions. Spoon the rest of

For the syrup
150 ml (5 fl oz/⅔ cup) water
100 g (3½ oz/½ cup) caster
  (superfine) sugar
50 ml (2 fl oz/¼ cup)
  elderflower cordial
50 ml (2 fl oz/¼ cup)
  St-Germain liqueur, or use
  extra elderflower cordial

the cream into a piping bag. Soak each of the pianono in the syrup then stand on a baking tray (pan). Pipe a ball of the cream onto the top of each of the pianono, sprinkle with sugar and then use a blow torch to caramelise the top, or you can pop under a very hot grill briefly. Leave to cool, then devour.

Yemas del Tajo

Serves 12–16

If you ever visit Málaga, you need to go to Ronda, a city with a long and varied history. Once there, you must try *yemas del Tajo* from Las Campanas at Plaza del Socorro; small cakes made of egg yolks and sugar. They are simple to make, however, this is only the case if you get three essential things right: the quality of the eggs, adding the eggs at the appropriate moment, and patience. Crack these, and you'll have a melt-in-the-mouth explosion of flavour.

150 ml (5 fl oz/⅔ cup) water
100 g (3½ oz/½ cup) caster (superfine) sugar
pared zest of 1 lemon
1 cinnamon stick
12 medium egg yolks
icing (confectioner's) sugar, for dusting

Put the water and the sugar into a saucepan with the lemon zest and cinnamon stick and gently dissolve over a low heat. Once dissolved, increase to a boil and cook for 7–10 minutes, until it reaches hard ball stage (160°C/320°F on a sugar thermometer). Remove the lemon and cinnamon.

Lightly beat the egg yolks then add these to the sugar syrup and cook over a medium-low heat, gently stirring all the time, for 3–4 minutes, until the mixture really thickens up and comes away from the edges of the pan.

Scoop onto a non-stick baking tray (pan) and spread out to cool, covering with a sheet of cling film (plastic wrap) to stop a skin forming. Once cold, dust a work surface thickly with icing (confectioner's) sugar. Use your fingers to break off small walnut-sized pieces of the mixture and drop them onto the sugar to coat. Roll into rough balls and put them into small paper cases. Chill in the fridge for at least 1 hour to form a crust, then serve.

Pan de higo

Serves 6

I have always wanted to write this recipe. *Pan de higo* is found all over Andalusia, but often it can be a bit hard and dry – adding some dried tropical fruit gives it a little bit more moisture and flavour. It sounds odd, but fantastic tropical fruits are grown along the Costa de Motril between Granada and Salobreña – a stunning road trip, and well worth doing.

400 g (14 oz) dried figs, roughly chopped
100 ml (3½ fl oz/scant ½ cup) brandy
200 g (7 oz) blanched almonds
100 g (3½ oz) mixed dried tropical fruit
2 tablespoons sesame seeds
½ teaspoon ground aniseed
pinch of cinnamon
pinch of dried cloves
1 tablespoon honey

To serve
hard cheese, such as manchego
honey, to drizzle

Place the figs and brandy in a small saucepan over a medium heat and warm through until steaming. Allow to cool, then drain the brandy from the figs and reserve in a bowl.

In a small frying pan, toast the almonds over a medium heat for 3–4 minutes, until golden. Tip into a food processor and whizz until they are finely chopped, but not quite a paste. Spoon into a mixing bowl and set aside.

Put the soaked figs and tropical fruit in the food processor and pulse to a rough paste. Add to the almonds and stir in the rest of the ingredients with just enough of the reserved brandy to hold the mixture together.

Spoon into 6 mini loaf tins, about 10 × 6 cm (4 × 2½ in) and 4 cm (1½ in) deep, pressing down well. Put a piece of baking paper on top of each tin, then stack the tins so they sit on top of each other. Place an empty tin and a heavy weight on top to compress the cakes.

Leave to dry for 3 days before removing the cakes from the tins and serving with cheese and a drizzle of honey.

Lola's pan de Calatrava

Serves 6

Pan means bread in Spanish; in order to make a simple flan go further in poorer households, bread was added, and so *pan de Calatrava* was born. Made with just eggs, milk and, of course, bread, it is both cheap and easy – something most families would be able to do at home. A friend of mine introduced me to Lola, from Baza, north of Granada, who generously shared this recipe with me, as she did not want it to get lost. This recipe is iconic in Mama Lola's family, and she normally makes this dessert for Christmas, Easter and all of her grandchildren's birthdays.

250 g (9 oz/1¼ cups) caster (superfine) sugar
300 g (10½ oz) stale bread or sponge cake, cut into 3 cm (1¼ in) cubes
500 ml (17 fl oz/2 cups) whole (full-fat) milk
1 cinnamon stick
4 large free-range eggs

Preheat the oven to 170°C (340°F/Gas 4).

Over a low heat, very gently melt half of the sugar in a wide frying pan, swirling every now and again to help it melt evenly. Once melted, allow it to bubble and turn a deep caramel colour. Remove from the heat and pour into the bottom of a 900 g (2 lb) non-stick loaf tin then top with the bread, pressing it down into an even layer. Set aside.

In a small saucepan over a medium heat, warm the milk with the cinnamon stick until steaming. Take off the heat and leave to infuse for 20 minutes, then remove the cinnamon.

In a medium mixing bowl, beat the eggs with the remaining sugar with an electric whisk until fluffy and light, then gradually stir in the cinnamon milk. Pour over the caramel and bread in the tin.

Place the loaf tin into a deep roasting tin, and pour boiling water around the outside so it comes about halfway up the sides. Gently slide into the oven and bake for 45 minutes– 1 hour, until just set.

Allow to cool for 1 hour before turning it out onto a plate, using a sharp knife to loosen the sides, then cut into slices and serve.

Pumpkin & chestnut fritters

**Makes 14 large patties
or 30 mini patties**

These fritters hail from northern Granada. In the past, when sugar was a valuable commodity and pretty expensive, they were a sweet treat for children on special occasions or bank holidays, which is why they are now typically served at Easter. Pumpkin might sound unusual in a dessert, but it was an abundant and versatile vegetable and therefore widely used.

1 × 425 g (15 oz) tin pumpkin purée
200 g (7 oz/1¾ cups) plain (all-purpose) flour
50 g (2 oz/⅓ cup) chestnut flour
100 g (3½ oz/½ cup) caster (superfine) sugar, plus extra for dusting
1½ teaspoons cinnamon, plus extra for dusting
¼ teaspoon sea salt
1 teaspoon baking powder
80 ml (2 fl oz/¼ cup) whole (full-fat) milk
3 large free-range eggs
olive oil, for frying

In a large mixing bowl, beat the pumpkin purée with the flours, sugar, cinnamon, salt, baking powder, milk and eggs until smooth.

Pour 2–3 cm (¾–1 in) olive oil into a deep frying pan over a medium heat until shimmering. Drop in tablespoonfuls of the mixture to make fourteen 8 cm (3¼ in) or thirty 6 cm (2¼ in) diameter patties. Fry for 2–3 minutes on each side until deep golden, then lift onto kitchen paper to drain. Allow to cool slightly.

Mix a spoonful each of cinnamon and sugar in a wide, shallow bowl. Dust the fritters in the sugar and serve.

Honey pastries with baked figs

Serves 10–12

This is my kind of dessert – packed with interesting flavours, and a stunning centrepiece for the table. It's hard to beat roasted figs, bursting with sweetness straight from the oven, with just a touch of soft goat's cheese and honey for balance.

125 g (4½ oz/⅔ cup) caster (superfine) sugar
50 ml (2 fl oz/¼ cup) honey
½ teaspoon orange blossom water
225 ml (7½ fl oz/scant 1 cup) water
150 g (5 oz) mixed nuts such as walnuts, almonds, pistachios, finely chopped
½ teaspoon ground cinnamon
100 g (3½ oz) unsalted butter, melted
6–8 sheets of filo pastry
crème fraîche (optional)

For the figs
8 ripe figs, halved
good drizzle of honey
4 tablespoons Pedro Ximénez sherry
handful of flaked almonds, toasted

To serve
crème fraîche

Preheat the oven to 180°C (350°F/Gas 4).

In a small saucepan, melt the sugar, honey and orange blossom water with the water, then simmer gently for 10–15 minutes, until slightly reduced and syrupy.

Mix the chopped nuts with the cinnamon. Lightly grease an 18–20 cm (7–8 in) square shallow tin with a little of the melted butter. Lay a sheet of filo in the bottom (trim if necessary) and brush with the butter, scatter with the nuts then add another layer of filo and melted butter. Repeat 4 times, ending with a final layer of filo. Butter the top generously and use a sharp knife to cut into diamond shapes. Bake for 25–30 minutes, until golden and crisp.

Spoon half of the cooled syrup over the pastries as they come out of the oven. Let stand for 5 minutes, then spoon over the rest of the syrup. Allow to cool completely in the tin.

As the pastries are cooling, place the figs in a small baking dish and drizzle with honey and sherry. Bake in the oven for 15–20 minutes until tender. Serve the pastries with the baked figs and a dollop of crème fraîche, if you like.

Churros

Serves 20–25

Churros are well known all over the world, but they are absolutely everywhere in Andalusia. Apparently it was originally a Chinese dish, brought to Spain by shipping merchants. Almost like a fried bread, they provided an alternative to fresh bread for shepherds when they were away in the mountains with their flocks of sheep. In fact, the name churros came from this, as the shape of them is very similar to churra sheep horns. It's common to serve these – or early in the morning, just before going to bed, as a final celebration for New Year's Eve or *férias*, after dancing the night away.

250 g (9 oz/2 cups) plain (all-purpose) flour
1 teaspoon baking powder
pinch of sea salt
320–350 ml (11–12 fl oz/ 1⅓–1½ cups) water
50 g (2 oz) unsalted butter, melted
1 litre (34 fl oz/4 cups) olive oil or sunflower oil, for frying
50 g (2 oz) caster (superfine) sugar
1 teaspoon ground cinnamon

Sift the flour, baking powder and salt into a mixing bowl. Put the butter and water into a saucepan and bring to the boil. Pour over the flour and beat until you have a thick but pipeable batter. Cover with cling film (plastic wrap) and chill for 20 minutes.

Heat the oil in a deep saucepan to 180°C (350°F) – or until a cube of bread browns in about 20 seconds. Fit a star nozzle to a large disposable piping bag and spoon the mixture into it. Once the oil is hot enough, pipe the mixture into the pan in long lines, using scissors to cut the batter when each churro is about 12 cm (4¾ in) long. Fry about 3 or 4 at a time for 3 minutes, until golden brown. Drain on kitchen paper.

Mix the sugar and cinnamon together in a shallow bowl and scatter over the top of the churros, or use to dip the ends into as you eat.

Roscos de huevo

Makes 60

Sor Natividad, one of the older nuns at the convent in Ronda, has spent her entire life cooking sweet things; she is 89 years old, and teaches her recipes to all the new nuns coming to the convent. Natividad was born and raised in Estepa, which has a reputation for having the best Christmas sweets and bakes, so her knowledge is unparalleled. I feel very privileged to have spent time with her, both cooking and tasting her food. Selling sweets, baked goods and desserts helps the nuns to generate income, as it's the only way they can maintain the convent – as an old building, it's very expensive to run.

125 ml (4¼ fl oz/½ cup) extra-virgin olive oil, plus extra for oiling
2 lemons: 1 zest pared; 1 zest finely grated
5 free-range eggs
500 g (1 lb 2 oz/2½ cups) caster (superfine) sugar, plus extra for dipping
3 tablespoons honey
800 g (1 lb 12 oz/4 cups) plain (all-purpose) flour
1 teaspoon ground cinnamon
½ × 7 g (¼ oz) sachet of yeast

Preheat the oven to 180°C (350°F/Gas 4). Line two baking trays (pans) with baking paper.

In a small saucepan over a medium-low heat, gently warm the oil with the pared lemon zest, then set aside to infuse for at least 15 minutes. Once infused, discard the lemon.

In a large bowl, beat the eggs with the sugar, honey and grated lemon zest. Stir in the infused olive oil. Sift the flour, cinnamon and yeast together over another bowl. Add half to the eggs and mix well, then add the rest and knead into a smooth, soft dough.

Very lightly oil your hands and break off pieces of dough, about 25 g (¾ oz) each, then roll them and shape into ring doughnuts. Dip the top in sugar, then place onto the prepared baking trays, sugared-side up.

Bake for 12–15 minutes, until golden and just cooked. Allow to cool on a wire rack, then serve.

Mantecados

Makes 12

400 g (14 oz/3⅔ cups) plain
    (all-purpose) flour
100 g (3½ oz/1 cup) almond
    flour
220 g (7¾ oz) lard
175 g (6 oz/¾ cup) icing
    (confectioner's) sugar, plus
    extra for dusting
1 teaspoon ground cinnamon

The name of this dessert comes from *manteca*, which means lardo, or lard, and it's the perfect biscuit with a mid-morning cup of tea. *Mantecados* have always been popular in my house – even for breakfast. My mum never used cinnamon in hers, but I do believe they are infinitely better with almonds.

Preheat the oven to 220°C (430°F/Gas 7).

Spread the plain flour on a baking tray (pan) and toast in the oven for a few minutes, until the top is beginning to turn lightly golden. Mix it up and then return to the oven and toast again. Do this 3–4 times until well toasted, but not burnt, and allow the flour to cool.

Mix the toasted flour with the almond flour in a food processor or in a deep bowl with an electric whisk. Add the lard and pulse to combine. Add the icing sugar and cinnamon and pulse again until the mixture starts to come together; if not using a food processor, beat together with a wooden spoon.

Tip out onto a clean work surface and bring together with your hands and lightly knead until smooth. It will be quite crumbly but should hold together. Shape into a disc and wrap in cling film (plastic wrap) and chill in the fridge for 20 minutes.

Preheat the oven to 180°C (350°F/Gas 4). Line a baking tray with baking paper.

On a floured work surface, roll out the dough to about 2½ cm (1 in) thick. Use a 6 cm (2½ in) round biscuit cutter to stamp out discs, then place on the baking tray. Reroll the trimmings to cut out as many as you can. Bake for 12–15 minutes, until just golden brown. Allow to cool on the tray for 10 minutes, then transfer to a wire rack to cool completely.

Sift over a light dusting of icing sugar before serving.

Alfajores with cardamom dulce de leche

Makes 20–25

It's easy to find a shop-bought dulce de leche and, yes, making your own does take time, but I promise the results are worth it. The cardamom adds a Moorish, aromatic flair; my partner Peter usually adds any left over to his black coffee.

125 g (4 oz) unsalted butter, softened
100 g (3½ oz/½ cup) caster (superfine) sugar
2 medium free-range egg yolks
finely grated zest of 1 lemon
1 teaspoon vanilla bean paste
100 g (3½ oz/⅔ cup) plain (all-purpose) flour, plus extra for dusting
150 g (5 oz/1¼ cups) cornflour (cornstarch)
1 teaspoon baking powder
desiccated coconut, for dusting

For the dulce de leche
1 litre (34 fl oz/4 cups) whole (full-fat) milk
300 g (10½ oz/1½ cups) caster (superfine) sugar
6 cardamom pods, cracked
¼ teaspoon bicarbonate of soda (baking soda)

First, make the dulce de leche. Place the milk, sugar and cardamom in a deep saucepan over a low heat and gently let the sugar melt. Once melted, increase the heat until it is almost boiling. Remove from the heat and whisk in the bicarbonate of soda. Return to the heat and bring back to a bubbling simmer, stirring often to stop it catching. You want the heat high enough to let the milk reduce and darken in colour but not stick to the pan. Simmer for 1–1 ½ hours, checking every 10 minutes or so, until you have a thick dark dulce de leche. Spoon into sterilised jars and cool completely; this will make more than you need for the alfajores, but will keep in a jar for 1 month.

To make the alfajores, beat the butter and sugar with an electric whisk in a medium bowl until light and fluffy. Beat in the egg yolks one at a time, then add the lemon zest and vanilla. Sift over the flours and baking powder and mix with a wooden spoon to form a smooth dough. Shape into a disc and wrap in cling film (plastic wrap) and chill for at least 1 hour in the fridge.

Line two baking trays (pans) with baking paper. Roll out the dough on a lightly floured surface to around ½ cm (¼ in) thick, then cut out about 50 rounds with a 5 cm (2 in) fluted biscuit cutter; you will need to reroll the trimmings. Place the rounds on the baking trays and chill for 20 minutes.

Preheat the oven to 180°C (350°F/Gas 4).

Take the trays out of the fridge and bake the biscuits for 7–8 minutes, until just cooked and a light golden brown. Leave to cool on the tray for 5 minutes, then transfer to a wire rack to cool completely.

Once the biscuits are cool, spread half of them with dulce de leche, then top with a second biscuit and roll the edges in the coconut.

Barbary fig margarita

Serves 2

In Spanish, they are called *higos chumbos*. Barbary figs or prickly pears are the fruit from cacti, and very popular all over Andalusia and the region that I'm from, Extremadura. I have to say I have always loved Barbary figs, but they've not always loved me – they are covered in tiny spikes, which get stuck all over my hands. In the town of Puerto de Santa María, there are two couples who sell them pre-peeled, which saves a lot of work. When I get them pre-prepared, I always think of the hard task I've avoided! This syrup will keep in the fridge for a few months.

100 ml (3⅓ fl oz/scant ½ cup)
    tequila
50 ml (2 fl oz/ ¼ cup) triple sec
50 ml (2 fl oz/ ¼ cup) Barbary
    fig syrup (see below)
juice of 1 lime, plus lime wedges
    to garnish
fine sea salt or caster
    (superfine) sugar, to garnish

For the Barbary fig syrup
1 kg (2 lb 3 oz) Barbary figs
    or prickly pears
800 g (1 lb 12 oz/4 cups) caster
    (superfine) sugar (depending
    on the amount of juice)
juice of 2 lemons

First, make the syrup. Place the whole figs in a saucepan, cover with water, bring to a boil then simmer very gently for 20 minutes. Mash the fruit well with a potato masher or blitz to a purée in a food processor. Pass through a fine mesh sieve into a jug, then strain again through a muslin (cheesecloth) into a jug or bowl. It should be a thin juice.

Measure the amount of the juice and pour into a saucepan. Add an equal amount of caster sugar and warm gently over a medium heat to dissolve the sugar, then simmer for 10 minutes, until it is a syrupy consistency. Add the lemon juice a little at a time to taste, then allow to cool. Pour into a sterilised bottle or jar; this will keep in the fridge for several months, and will make more than you need.

To make the cocktails, fill a cocktail shaker with ice and add the tequila, triple sec, syrup and lime juice and shake well. Run a lime wedge around the edge of 2 cocktail glasses and dip the rims in salt or sugar. Strain the margarita into the glasses and serve.

Andalusian menus

MENU 1
Serves 6

Strawberry gazpacho (page 176)

Tenderloin with pears & hazelnuts (page 61)

Beetroot, blood orange, pomegranate & manchego salad with membrillo dressing (page 130)

Honey pastries with baked figs (page 214)

THE DAY BEFORE

Make the honey pastries, cool, cover and store in a cool place overnight.

Put all the ingredients for the gazpacho in a bowl to marinate overnight.

Sear the loin and place in a dish to marinate overnight.

Roast and prep the beetroot and oranges and keep in bowls in the fridge.

ON THE DAY

Blend the gazpacho.

Make the dressing for the salad.

Slice the pears and roast the hazelnuts for the pork.

Bake the figs.

MENU 2
Serves 6

Oxtail croquetas (page 20)

Roast chicken with orange, cumin & apricot rice (page 47)

Jeannie's marmalade soufflé puddings with candied oranges (page 192)

TWO DAYS BEFORE

Make the slow-cooked oxtail (page 18), set aside enough for the croquetas and freeze the rest for another day.

Make the béchamel for the croquetas.

Make the candied oranges.

THE DAY BEFORE

Mix the oxtail and the béchamel together, shape into croquetas and chill.

Egg and breadcrumb the croquetas and freeze.

Make the marinade for the chicken and rub under the skin.

ON THE DAY

Make the soufflé mixture and chill until ready to cook.

Cook the chicken and rice.

Cook the croquetas from frozen, adding a couple of extra minutes to the cooking time.

MENU 3

Serves 6–8

Cheese-stuffed fried olives (page 159)

Aubergines with chestnut honey (page 133)

Artichokes, jamón Ibérico ham & egg yolk
(page 171)

Pipirrana (page 137)

Apricot sorbet with tejas dulces de Sevilla
(page 191)

TWO DAYS BEFORE

Make the sorbet and freeze.

Make the tejas and store in an airtight
container.

THE DAY BEFORE

Prepare the tomatoes, chillies and peppers
for the pipirrana.

Prepare the artichokes and leave in lemon
water overnight.

ON THE DAY

Stuff and fry the olives.

Prepare and fry the aubergines.

Cook the eggs and finish the pipirrana.

Cook the artichokes and finish the dish.

MENU 4

Serves 4, with leftover pionono

Tuna tartar (page 124)

Grilled octopus with asparagus, broad beans
& blackened lemon (page 113)

Santa Fé pionono with elderflower (page 202)

THE DAY BEFORE

Cook the octopus and remove the tentacles.

Make the cream for the pionono, spoon into
a piping bag and chill.

Make the syrup for the pionono and chill.

ON THE DAY

Make the sponge for the pionono and assemble.

Make the tartar.

Finish the octopus dish, griddle the vegetables
and octopus and assemble.

Places to eat in Andalusia

Seville

Bodeguita Romero
Calle Harinas, 10,
41001 Sevilla

Bodega Santa Cruz
Calle Rodrigo Caro, 1,
41004 Sevilla

La Moneda
Calle Almirantazgo, 4,
41001 Sevilla

Bajo Guia
Calle Adriano, 5,
41001 Sevilla

Cádiz

La Carboná
Calle San Francisco de
   Paula, 2,
11401 Jerez de la Frontera

La Duquesa
Carretera A-396 km 7700,
11170 Medina-Sidonia

El Campero
Avd. Constitucion, Local 5 C,
11160 Barbate

El Antonio
Bahía de la Plata, Atlanterra,
11393 Zahara de los Atunes

Casa Bigote
Calle Pórtico Bajo de Guía, 10,
11540 Sanlúcar de Barrameda

Cataria
Avenida Amilcar Baca, 14,
11139 Urb. Novo Santi Petri

El Faro del Puerto
Av. Fuenterrabía, km. 0.5,
11500 El Puerto de Sta María

La Castilleria
Sta. Lucía, s/n,
11150 Vejer de la Frontera

Aponiente
C/ Francisco Cossi Ochoa, s/n,
11500 El Puerto de Sta María

Huelva

Acanthum
Calle San Salvador, 17,
21003 Huelva

Finca Buenvino
21208 Los Marines, Huelva

José Vicente
Av. de Andalucía, 53,
21200 Aracena, Huelva

Granada

Las Tinajas
Calle Martínez Campos, 17,
18002 Granada

La Tana
Placeta del Agua, 3,
18009 Granada

Málaga

El Almocabar
Plaza Ruedo Alameda, 5,
29400 Ronda

Restaurante Skina
Calle Aduar, 12,
29601 Marbella

Lobito del Mar
Chef Dani García
Av. Bulevar Príncipe Alfonso
   de Hohenlohe, 178,
29602 Marbella

La Cosmopolita Malagueña
Calle José Denis Belgrano, 3,
29015 Málaga

Córdoba

Noor
Calle Pablo Ruiz Picasso, 8,
14014 Córdoba

Jaén

Baga
Calle Reja de la Capilla, 3,
23001 Jaén

Acknowledgements

Another book, another great adventure! As ever, it's all down to a great team. To Peter, as always, for your unconditional support, and to Zoraida – without you, this book would not have been possible. Thank you for your patience and assistance.

Thanks to Borra and Kate for believing in me; Kate as usual, it was wonderful to work you and your team.

Lizzie, I appreciate you putting my ideas into perfect English – I know that it's not that easy.

Emma, your stunning photos always feel like a luxury, and bring me back to great moments whenever I look at them. Thank you for all the driving!

To Clare for the great design and Daniel for the beautiful illustrations, and to Aya, for the lovely cooking on photoshoots. Tabitha, your prop styling really brings the colours, textures and light of Andalusia to life in the book.

To Maria Castro and the 5J team, I so appreciate your generous support and, of course, the incredible quality of the products.

Everyone in Huerta de Albalá cellars, and especially Vicente and Anne – with the creation of the winery, you've also created a large group of friends.

To Andrés and Yolanda, for sharing your knowledge about the area and your generosity with your time.

To Finca Buenvino: Jeanne and Sam, it was a pleasure to spend time in your home, doing what we really like, and having great talks around the table. And, of course, thank you to the wonderful Jago and Charlie.

To the Franciscan sisters of Ronda, and in particular to Madre Superior Nieves for opening the doors of your convent and giving us the opportunity to see your hundreds-of-years-old cookbook. In addition, thank you to Carlos Gracia for making this possible – I am so grateful.

To my friend Shawn, who took me to her favourite places in Seville, and really introduced me to the good vibes of the city. Thank you to each and every one of the restaurants I visited, and to your hardworking teams.

To all the team at the restaurants for helping me all year round and making so many people happy. I love you all.

Finally, to Junta de Andalucía: thank you for all your help, and the Spanish Tourist Office in the UK.

About the author

José Pizarro has lived in the UK for 20 years and in that time has worked at some of London's most prestigious Spanish restaurants including Eyre Brothers, Brindisa and Gaudi.

He owns three restaurants in London – José, Pizarro and José Pizarro. In 2019, José is opening The Swan Inn in Esher, a country pub with an à la carte menu, which will feature pub classics alongside regional Spanish dishes.

In 2014 José was voted one of '100 españoles' – a hugely prestigious award, which showcases the top 100 Spaniards around the world, based on how they have brought their talents to the masses and demonstrated their Spanish pride through their work.

Index